Gambling

Look for these and other books in the Lucent Overview Series:

Abortion
Acid Rain
Adoption
Advertising
Alcoholism
Animal Rights
Artificial Organs
The Beginning of Writing
The Brain
Cancer
Censorship
Child Abuse
Children's Rights
Cities
The Collapse of the Soviet Union
Cults
Dealing with Death
Death Penalty
Democracy
Drug Abuse
Drugs and Sports
Drug Trafficking
Eating Disorders
Elections
Endangered Species
The End of Apartheid in South Africa
Energy Alternatives
Espionage
Ethnic Violence
Euthanasia
Extraterrestrial Life
Family Violence
Gangs
Garbage
Gay Rights
Genetic Engineering
The Greenhouse Effect
Gun Control
Hate Groups
Hazardous Waste
The Holocaust

Homeless Children
Homelessness
Illegal Immigration
Illiteracy
Immigration
Juvenile Crime
Memory
Mental Illness
Militias
Money
Ocean Pollution
Oil Spills
The Olympic Games
Organ Transplants
Ozone
The Palestinian-Israeli Accord
Pesticides
Police Brutality
Population
Poverty
Prisons
Rainforests
The Rebuilding of Bosnia
Recycling
The Reunification of Germany
Schools
Smoking
Space Exploration
Special Effects in the Movies
Sports in America
Suicide
The UFO Challenge
The United Nations
The U.S. Congress
The U.S. Presidency
Vanishing Wetlands
Vietnam
Women's Rights
World Hunger
Zoos

Gambling

by Gail B. Stewart

Lucent
Books

Library of Congress Cataloging-in-Publication Data

Stewart, Gail, 1949-
  Gambling / by Gail B. Stewart.
      p. cm. — (Lucent overview series)
  Includes bibliographical references and index.
    ISBN 1-56006-765-9 (alk. paper)
    1. Gambling—United States—Juvenile literature. 2. Compulsive
  gambling—United States—Juvenile literature. [1. Gambling.]
  I. Title.   II. Series.
    HV6715 .S83 2001
    306.4'82'0973—dc21
                                                            00-011397

Copyright © 2001 by Lucent Books, Inc.
P.O. Box 289011, San Diego, CA 92198-9011
Printed in the U.S.A.

Contents

Introduction

THE EIGHTEEN-YEAR-OLD high school senior is a bit reluctant to discuss his gambling at first, but gradually warms to the topic. He has been playing poker with friends from school since he was thirteen or so, but admits that his taste for gambling action has expanded since then.

"I play with different guys now," he says. "Sometimes I play with people I know, but other times someone gives me the name of a guy who likes to play for high stakes, you know. And I give him a call, and I get in a game.

"When I used to play, like back years ago, we'd play for dimes and nickels. A really big pot for us was like three or four bucks. Now I play for way more money—it's kind of embarrassing to talk about."

He shrugs. "Maybe five hundred or so. I've been in a game that was over nine, but I [was out] by then. I just watched these three guys. I've won four hundred once in a night, but only once did I ever win that much. And I've lost three hundred in a weekend."

He insists that he will not tell his parents about his poker games, because he knows they would neither approve nor understand.

"They'd have been mad if they'd known about the three- or four- buck pots when I was in eighth grade," he says. "They'd go crazy if they knew about what I play for now. So far I've been able to cover all my losses, so there's been no need to go to them. I just tell them I'm going to a basketball game or something with my friends, and that I'll be out really late. They believe me."[1]

"It's not like I'm gambling away the baby's dinner"

Across town, Barbara, a seventy-six-year-old retired teacher, buys five lottery tickets as she pays for gasoline. She says she buys five each week.

"It's like clockwork for me," she laughs. "I use the birthdays of my grandchildren for my numbers, or my wedding anniversary, or my old address when I lived in Wisconsin— I just do whatever seems right. You get a hunch, you know, and you go with it.

"I've never won, but I've been right on two of the numbers once," she says. "That was really exciting—for about five seconds. Oh, you don't have to tell me how slim the chances are of winning! I know all that! But it's only a few dollars, and it's fun. I say, why not?

A Chicago police officer purchases a lottery ticket at a convenience store. Playing the lottery is just one of many ways to gamble.

"Life's short, and when the pot carries over to the next week, I just think, 'Boy, somebody's going to win.' And I can't think of any reason why that somebody couldn't be me. It's not like I'm gambling away the baby's dinner or anything. It's just for fun, just like going to a movie or something."[2]

"That teensy little hope"

Monica and her three sisters would wholeheartedly agree with Barbara's views. The three women have traveled almost two hundred miles to the Mystic Lake Casino near Minneapolis, and are eager to begin their weekend of gambling.

"We get together once every year or so," says Monica. "We live pretty close, but we are all busy with families and kids, church stuff—you name it. So we make a date to come down for two days and a night and gamble. I play blackjack, [sister] Eileen does the slot machines, and Karen kind of tries everything.

"None of us loses more than we can afford; we usually each bring about $200, and we all expect to go home without it! It's the fun of it—and if you've never tried blackjack or roulette or something, you don't know how much fun it can be. It's a rush when you win, even if it's just once in a while. The first time Eileen played a slot machine, she won five dollars, and you'd think she'd won a million, she was so excited.

"I guess we could all come down here and just use our money to go to the Mall of America or something, but that wouldn't be as much fun. I mean, shopping—you know you're going to lose your money. But in gambling, you always have that teensy little hope that you could come home with a lot more. That's the fun, I guess—and who does it hurt?"[3]

Gambling's shady image

Generations ago, the notion of gambling was far less lighthearted. The word gambling might evoke pictures of a cagey riverboat cardsharp or a smoke-filled betting parlor run by characters of questionable repute. Gamblers were often per-

ceived as get-rich-quick schemers, and the casinos they visited as nests of drinking and prostitution.

Such images have little to do with gambling's legality or illegality; though gambling in various forms has been legal for much of U.S. history, its image often has been shady. As one expert points out, "Not that long ago, Americans held gambling in nearly the same esteem as heroin dealing and applauded when ax-wielding police paid a visit to the corner dice room."[4]

In past years, many Americans worried that the lure of gambling was so strong that it could have dangerous results. Stories abounded of people who gambled away their life savings and became destitute overnight. Parents warned their children to stay away from pool halls and bars where gamblers gathered.

Children were not the only ones deemed in need of protection. In 1955 baseball commissioner Ford Frick so feared the

Government agents destroy slot machines in Chicago in 1910, a time when gambling was considered lurid and dangerous.

corruption inherent in betting that to protect the integrity of the game, he prohibited all major league ball players from staying overnight in Las Vegas, the nation's gambling capital.

"America's pastime"

Today, gambling (or "gaming," as casino owners call it now) has a far different look. Far from being isolated in the deserts of Nevada or in back rooms in big cities like New York and Chicago, gambling is open and easy. Casinos, once found only in Las Vegas and Atlantic City, New Jersey, now operate in most states, and many of them project a "family-friendly" image. Lotteries and racetracks abound, too; today every state except Utah and Hawaii allows some form of legal gambling.

Gambling is not merely legal, it is a part of everyday life; it is not merely tolerated, it is encouraged. So prevalent is it, in fact, that Americans bet $600 billion in 1998 and lost

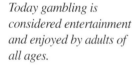

Today gambling is considered entertainment and enjoyed by adults of all ages.

about $60 billion in lotteries, at casinos, bingo halls, or racetracks, or online in gambling's newest form, the Internet casino. That means that Americans spent more on gambling than they did on movies, sporting events, theme parks, cruise ships, and recorded music combined.

The faces of today's gamblers are diverse—teens, senior citizens, and everyone in between. Those reluctant to attend a casino or racetrack can find bingo games at neighborhood churches and schools, organized as fund-raisers. "We couldn't think of a better way to raise money for our kids to attend a leadership convention in New York," says one priest. "We raised far more than we'd dreamed."[5]

It seems that gambling has become America's national pastime, an observation that would not have surprised humorist Will Rogers, who generations ago noted that people in the United States enjoyed the risk and daring of wagering money. "There is," said Rogers, "a wide gambling streak in nearly every American man and woman—a fat streak, fat as hog's bacon."[6]

Thorny questions

But however popular and acceptable gambling has become—and however diverse its participants—many people question its effects on society. Some point to an increasing rate of compulsive gambling, especially among teens, and worry that easy access to casinos is too much of a temptation for people who simply cannot afford to lose money. Some are concerned with how the influx of casinos affects the community; they argue that gambling merely redistributes funds instead of spurring genuine economic growth, and worry that gambling invites crime, organized or not. Others feel that gambling undermines the work ethic and makes people look for easy riches.

There are staunch defenders of gambling, too—including government officials—who maintain that without gambling revenues, states would have to tax far more heavily than they do now. Defenders also point to Native American reservations, where casinos have brought in staggering amounts of money to finance tribal schools, health care, and preschool programs that would rival any in mainstream upper-class neighborhoods.

None of these claims is easily dismissed. However, by looking at the background of gambling in the United States, as well as at its blossoming as America's pastime over the past few years, it is easier to understand the scope of the issue and how it has become a divisive topic today.

1

Our Gambling Heritage

ONE ASPECT OF gambling that is *not* debated is its long history. People have been wagering and gambling throughout the world for thousands of years. The ancient Romans bet on the outcome of gladiator matches and chariot races. The ancient Greeks made dice from the knucklebones of sheep or cows, and played a variety of wagering games. The early Egyptians played dice games, too; ornate dice made of ivory and bone have been found in some of the pharaohs' tombs.

Through the centuries, people invented many games that involved a combination of chance and skill. By the 1300s, dice and card games were particularly popular, as was betting on horse races. By the time Columbus and his crew set out for the New World, it is estimated that there were more than one hundred popular games on which people liked to gamble.

Gambling comes to America

The earliest settlers who came to America from Europe brought many of their favorite games with them. Dice and cards helped pass the time in the evenings and during cold winter days when little could be done outside.

But as popular as the games were among the settlers, some citizens voiced concerns. They worried that long gambling games were often accompanied by heavy drinking and rough language. They worried, too, about time wasted at

A Roman emperor and empress decide the fate of contestants in a gladiator match. Wagering on the outcomes of sporting events and other games has been around for centuries.

cards that could be better spent doing other things—including going to church. In the Dutch settlement of New Amsterdam, for example, many were playing backgammon during church services. That activity prompted a law prohibiting gambling during church, a move that seemed to solve the problem there.

The Puritan leaders of Plymouth Colony were more disapproving. They called gambling "the Devil's work" and playing cards "the Devil's picture book." They passed several laws prohibiting gambling in 1656; the punishment for the first offense was a fine of forty shillings; additional offenses drew a public whipping.

Although many critics of gambling were ministers, members of the clergy were sometimes gamblers, too. In the Virginia Assembly, lawmakers in 1624 admonished that "Mynisters shall not give themselves to excesse in drinking or yett spend their tyme idelie by day or night, playing at dice, cards, or any unlawful game."[7]

Immune to laws?

Although many laws prohibited various types of gambling during the seventeenth century, it seemed that people were quite willing to risk fines or other punishment to continue. Cards and dice were available in nearly every roadside tavern, as well as in many homes. It was impossible for local authorities to enforce the laws, so most offenders went unpunished.

Gambling was a popular habit among some of the most famous Americans of the eighteenth century. George Washington, for example, was said to have bet on horse racing

Even President Washington enjoyed gambling, but he was pressured by the legislature to ban it throughout the Continental Army.

and dice, and enjoyed nothing better on a rainy afternoon than gambling at cards. Washington kept a careful journal of his wins and losses; his entry for January 18, 1768, reads, "At home all day at cards—it [was] snowing. . . . By cash set aside for card money, five pounds."[8]

Thomas Jefferson, too, enjoyed gambling. He and his wife played backgammon and lotto (a game of chance like bingo) and agreed that the games were far more interesting when money was at stake. However, Jefferson strongly advocated moderation in gambling, concerned that serious habitual wagering could lead to problems in society.

Jefferson pointed out that habitual gamblers frequently wagered more than they could afford to lose; losing money that should be spent on feeding and sheltering their families was irresponsible. Such unbridled gambling, he warned, "corrupts our dispositions, and teaches us a habit of hostility against all mankind."[9]

Warnings of trouble

Jefferson's concerns might have been warranted, at least in regard to General Washington's Continental Army. Gambling in the ranks was rampant; the Virginia House of Burgesses, hearing rumors of the widespread wagering, warned Washington that he would lose the support of the legislature unless he could control the problem.

Washington's attempted solution was to ban all gambling, especially after the Revolutionary War began. It was then that he ordered "all officers, noncommissioned officers and soldiers . . . positively forbid playing at cards, or other games of chance. . . . At this time of public distress, men must find enough to do, in the service of their God and country, without abandoning themselves to vice and immorality."[10]

The men under his command were said to have greatly respected Washington, but they were reluctant to give up one of their only ways of passing time during the long winter months. It was during the most difficult of times that wagering was most common. At Valley Forge, for example, where soldiers had little to eat and were sick and freezing, betting helped improve low morale.

The favorite betting game was called "toss up," in which the men wagered on the landing position of a handful of coins thrown into the air. As one historian notes, "No one could stop a game so simple that it required only spare change and boredom, not where both were in good supply."[11]

The lottery

One form of gambling that emerged early in the nation's history, however, met with less opposition than dice or cards did. It was the lottery, a game that worked very much like lotteries run by individual states today. People bought numbered tickets for a relatively small amount of money in hopes that their ticket would be pulled out of a hat in a random drawing, thereby winning a cash prize.

Although playing the lottery was considered gambling, it was less objectionable to many people in the seventeenth and eighteenth centuries. Lottery players did not congregate in taverns for hours on end, nor did the lottery lead to excessive drinking and swearing. A great many people played the lottery, from chronic card players to esteemed members of the clergy. In a 1764 journal entry, the highly respected Rev. Samuel Seabury writes:

> The ticket No. 5866 in the Light House and Public Lottery of New York, drew in my favor, by the blessing of Almighty God, 599 pounds sterling, of which I received 425 pounds, there being a deduction of fifteen percent; for which I now record to my posterity my thanks and praise to Almighty God, the giver of all good gifts.[12]

Money-raising potential

But perhaps the most attractive aspect of the lottery was its tremendous money-making potential for the organizers—whether a city, church, or group of individuals. Because the lottery always took in more money than it gave out in prizes, a hefty sum could be raised quite quickly.

The first lottery benefiting people in America was actually held in Europe. Historians say that the Jamestown settlement in early-seventeenth-century Virginia would almost certainly have failed had it not been for a lottery.

Jamestown was established in 1607; however, by 1612 the settlers had undergone hard times and were ready to return to Europe. Supporters in England organized a lottery, and the proceeds were enough to send two well-stocked ships to the settlement, relieving shortages and making it possible for the settlers to remain.

As America grew, lotteries were held to finance some of its most pressing needs. In 1746, Benjamin Franklin organized a lottery in Philadelphia to raise nearly £3,000; the money was needed for military supplies during the French and Indian War. Another took place decades later to outfit the Continental Army that would fight the British in the Revolutionary War.

"A salutary instrument"

After the Revolutionary War, lotteries were even more popular. Taxation had been an explosive issue between the

According to historians, it was the money raised by a lottery held in Europe that saved the settlement in Jamestown, Virginia (pictured), in the early seventeenth century.

colonists and the British. The new American government knew how suspiciously citizens would view any attempt to levy a tax; thus, legislators were reluctant to impose any taxes at all.

However, money was sorely needed to finance basic building projects. A lottery seemed a far more pleasant solution, for it was both voluntary, and full of possibilities for ticket buyers to win something. And the plan was successful. According to one historian, "From the proceeds of this wholesale gambling, churches were built, colleges founded, and endowed; and roads, bridges, canals, and other public works were constructed."[13]

In fact, say experts, many of the most beautiful and historic buildings in the eastern United States were built with lottery money. Such prestigious academic institutions as Harvard, Yale, and Dartmouth were kept afloat with money from lotteries, as well.

Thomas Jefferson, who had denounced other types of gambling for the dangers they posed, called the lottery "a salutary [beneficial] instrument," and explained that whenever money was needed for something, it could be "raised therefore by a lottery, wherein the tax is laid on the willing only, that is to say, on those who can risk the price of a ticket without sensible injury."[14]

The growth of the lottery

By the end of the eighteenth century, more than two thousand lotteries operated in the United States. Lists of drawings and prizes were published daily in the newspapers; there were so many that the list is said to have required a half-column of fine print in the New York papers alone. The largest lotteries, in New York and Philadelphia, generated more than $2 million per year in each city—a fact that pleased city governments immensely.

However, with the increase of lottery gambling came corruption. While most of the lotteries were run honestly (usually by private companies), growing evidence suggested that

By the end of the eighteenth century, lotteries were extremely popular and huge crowds would gather to see who won.

some lotteries were not. Some lottery organizers were selling tickets and simply leaving town before the prizes could be awarded. Others sold tickets to lotteries that did not really exist. Still others sold a great many tickets and paid off with a ridiculously small prize.

Frauds, scams, and the end of the lottery

One infamous example of the latter was the Plymouth Lottery, approved by the Massachusetts legislature to raise money to improve Plymouth's beach. The lottery had been in operation for nine years before someone noted that in that time only $9,876 had been turned over by lottery promoters—who had in that same period pocketed almost $1 million for themselves.

Another swindle that fueled public outrage occurred in Washington, D.C., in 1823. Congress had authorized a Grand National Lottery that would benefit the city, and tens of thousands of tickets had been sold. The winning number, belonging to a Virginia man named Clarke, was to pay $100,000. However, before the prize was awarded, the promoter of the lottery fled with hundreds of thousands of dollars. Clarke sued, and after four years of lawsuits, the courts agreed that the city of Washington was liable for the amount.

As more and more abuses were uncovered, pressure to ban lotteries altogether intensified. A New York grand jury investigating the many lotteries in that state agreed in 1830 that "as now managed, [lotteries] are an evil of the most alarming nature, both in a moral and pecuniary point of view."[15] State by state, lotteries were banned. By the beginning of the Civil War in 1861, there were no legal lotteries left in the United States.

The lottery did make a comeback in the South immediately after the Civil War as a means of raising money for reconstruction. The most successful Southern lottery was in Louisiana. Nicknamed "the Serpent," it awarded huge cash prizes, but still made more than $13 million each year, largely through ticket sales conducted by mail to citizens of other states.

As were other lotteries before it, the Serpent was misused by greedy organizers. It became a cash cow for corrupt politicians, too; many lawmakers made deals with lottery organizers to receive a share of its enormous profits in return for political favors. It eventually was put out of business when President Benjamin Harrison asked Congress to pass a national law forbidding lottery tickets from being sold through the mail.

The riverboat gamblers

Though it was no longer legal to gamble in lotteries between 1830 and the beginning of the Civil War, there were plenty of other options for wagering during the period. True, statutes in many states still prohibited gambling on dice and card games, but almost anyone could find a back-room game if he looked hard enough. Besides, many police officers enjoyed poker, too—and could often be persuaded to look the other way when such illegal activities occurred in their towns.

Since there were no laws restricting it, gambling was widespread on Mississippi riverboats in the 1800s.

Some of the most exciting gambling was done on large riverboats that made their way on the Mississippi River, connecting the bustling towns of Memphis, Cincinnati, St. Louis, and New Orleans. Many riverboat passengers were planters and businessmen who usually had a great deal of money with them and very little to do on the trip. Because state laws did not bind river trade, gambling was open and widespread.

The bulging wallets of the passengers attracted professional gamblers to the riverboats—people who had no reason to buy a ticket other than to play cards. Historians say that between 1820 and 1860, there were 735 riverboats in operation, and more than 2,000 professional gamblers were making their living on them. These gamblers were regarded with scorn by early riverboat crews, who considered them cheats and lowlifes, far beneath the ordinary passenger. When a riverboat accident in 1817 killed eleven passengers, for instance, one survivor wrote in his journal, "Among them was a gambler, who was buried separately."[16]

But as time went on, the captains realized that the gamblers were steady customers who provided a diversion for other passengers on the long river journeys. (Too, some of the most dishonest cardsharps made agreements to share some of their winnings with cooperative captains and crews.) And many travelers were eager to sit down at lavishly appointed poker tables to try their luck with professional gamblers.

Embroidered vests and gold chains

The gamblers were usually easy to spot, for they spent much of their winnings on clothes and jewelry for themselves. They favored black clothing, ruffled white shirts, and elegant, jewel-toned vests. The vest was, says one historian, "the place for color . . . for the art of embroidery. Signs and omens of luck, hounds and horses in full action, glowing patterns, even whole landscapes could march across a gambler's waistcoat."[17]

Their coat buttons were often gold or silver, sometimes inlaid with pearls or other gems. The favorite piece of jewelry, however, seemed to be the massive gold watches most carried in their pockets. Such a timepiece could cost $1,000—an unbelievable amount in those days—set with diamonds in its stem. The watches were attached to chains that were sometimes as gaudy as the watches themselves—often as thick as a pencil. One gambler named Jimmy Fitzgerald, reputed to be one of the biggest dandies on the riverboats, had a chain that was almost twenty feet long and looped several times around his neck.

"The fellows had to be pretty slick"

While some riverboat gamblers might have been honest, the vast majority were not. Yet they were so skilled that it was almost impossible for an onlooker to detect cheating. Often they used decks of cards that had been doctored, or marked, so that they could easily tell what cards another player held. Sometimes they relied on shuffling and dealing sleight-of-hand moves that they had perfected.

One riverboat gambler confessed long afterward that playing with honest card players was more like robbery than gambling, because the cheaters were so smooth:

> The fellows had to be pretty slick, I can tell you. . . . I've seen fellows pick every card in a pack, and call it without missing once. I've seen them shuffle them one for one all through from top to bottom, so that they were in the same position after a few dozen shuffles that they were in at first. They'd just flutter them up like a flock of quail and get the aces, kings, queens, jacks, and tens all together as easy as pie. A sucker had no more chance against those fellows than a snowball in a red-hot oven.[18]

Besides the dandy with his gold chains and fancy suits there were very successful cardsharps who worked in groups of from three to six. They boarded the boat at different stops and pretended not to know one another. When one of them got into a poker game, his allies would either deal him winning cards or "telegraph" to him the contents of the other players' hands with hand signals or even puffs of cigar smoke. One accomplice, who pretended to be a musi-

cian striding about the saloon, actually played signals on his violin.

Gambling and drinking in saloons were part of life in the frontier towns of the American West.

Gambling in the West

Gambling among the exploding population of the American West was as popular as it was on the riverboats. While many states east of the Mississippi had enacted laws either banning or limiting gambling, the westward expansion of the United States had opened up new settlements and towns in which those laws did not apply. In frontier towns, gambling and drinking in the local saloons were two of the few pleasures available in an otherwise hard life.

In Kansas cattle towns like Dodge City and Abilene, gambling was everywhere, every hour of the day (and night). And just as it was on the riverboats, the presence of cowboys fresh off the trail with money in their pockets was a magnet for cardsharps and con men eager to help them lose it.

Farther west, the California gold rush sparked an explosion of gambling activity, too. Money was made quickly, and often lost even more quickly at the poker and dice tables; betting $20,000 on a single hand or throw was not uncommon. Researcher Ann Fabian suggests why newly wealthy prospectors and miners wagered so freely: "Money was not earned in slow and steady toil; it fell suddenly, like manna. And the miners who won their money in lucky windfalls turned and gambled their profits on unlikely wagers."[19]

Gambling houses

Nowhere during that time was gambling more prevalent than in San Francisco. Shrewd businessmen opened gambling houses, or casinos, where games of every sort were played twenty-four hours a day. Casinos were nothing new, of course; plenty were in existence in big cities in the East and Midwest, fancy houses with felt-edged tables, wonderful food, and whiskey served in crystal glasses.

The casinos of San Francisco were far more spartan. They were often no more than a large tent with sawdust on the floor. There were no lovely oak tables or sumptuous menus; the gamblers usually lined up outside, waiting for a turn to play. By 1855 there were more than one thousand such casinos along San Francisco's waterfront, known as the Barbary Coast.

Like the saloons of the Old West, the casinos were often dangerous places, for fights and gunplay were rampant. Anyone discovered to be cheating was usually taken out by those he had wronged, shot, and dragged into an alley or thrown off a wharf into the sea. City newspapers frequently warned citizens of the dangers of being in the gambling neighborhoods after dark.

But no matter how rough the company in the casinos and saloons, the western half of the United States was experiencing a gambling fever the likes of which had not been seen before. With poker games that never ended and stakes that often defied belief, it must have seemed in the latter half of the nineteenth century as though gambling was a fact of life that was surely here to stay.

2

The Dawn of Gambling's Modern Age

ALTHOUGH IT WAS thriving in the West, gambling seemed to be moving in the other direction in the rest of the United States. Because gambling often was accompanied by violence and drinking, more and more people were speaking out against it as immoral. Supported by civic and church leaders, opponents were able to put a great deal of pressure on lawmakers to ban or limit gambling in its various forms.

"An archaic trait"

Lotteries had already been banned from every state in the eastern half of the country. Horse racing had been limited to a handful of states, and the betting that went with it had been outlawed in most of those states. Under public pressure, the gambling houses and casinos that had become popular in cities like New Orleans, New York, and Washington, D.C.— some of which were elegant establishments frequented by politicians—were being forced to close their doors, too.

So much had been done to control gambling, in fact, that the antigambling public felt that their efforts had dealt a deathblow to the gambling world throughout the East. Gamblers were completely out of date in the modern world, one nineteenth-century economist declared:

> The gambling propensity is another subsidiary trait of the barbarian temperament. But in any case it is to be taken as an archaic

trait, inherited from a more or less remote past, more or less in-
compatible with the requirements of the industrial process, and
more or less of a hindrance to the fullest efficiency of the collec-
tive economic life of the present.[20]

Not gone, just harder to see

Yet while many opponents of gambling were congratulat-
ing themselves on a job well done, they were probably un-
aware that the gambling world had simply gone underground.
Gambling was illegal, just as prostitution was illegal; however, gambling continued as prostitution did, in a more secre-
tive, less visible manner.

Though betting on horse racing was illegal almost everywhere, there were still bookmakers glad to place one's bets at

*Even first-class
gambling houses
frequented by the upper
class were forced to
close their doors due to
public pressure.*

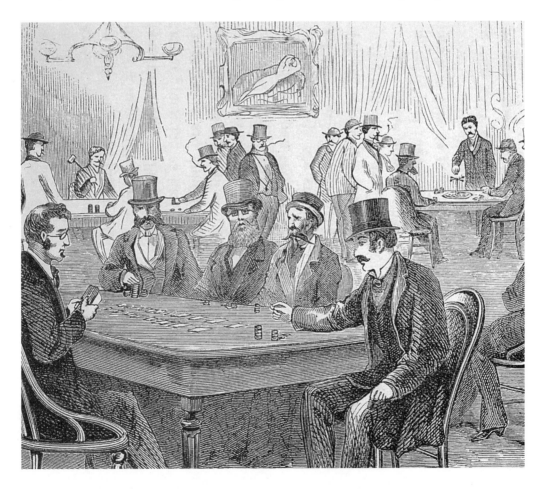

the track—for a cut of the profits. Poker and dice games still flourished, too, often in the backrooms of bars or restaurants. This went on either without police knowledge or, more likely, because local law enforcement officials were bribed to look the other way.

Even a widespread gambling game like the lottery continued to take place on a weekly basis in many cities. In New York, the lottery had been illegal since 1834, yet a local investigation in 1851 found that there were certain offices that "are well known to the police as places for the sale of lottery tickets, and yet they are suffered [allowed] to continue their mysterious operations."[21]

Even after that investigation turned up massive evidence of wrongdoing and officials were urged to take a more aggressive stance against the lottery dealers, lotteries continued. A New York journalist wrote in 1872 that "there is scarcely a street in the whole city, from the Battery to Harlem Bridge, where the shops of the lottery dealers cannot be found."[22]

Extending the ban

As the twentieth century began, similar public pressure to ban gambling in the western part of the country mounted. No longer were these areas considered frontiers dominated by a male population of cowboys and miners. By 1900 the towns and settlements of the West were attracting families. Says one historian, "The frontier retreated at an accelerated pace before the relentless march of the true town tamers, the permanent settlers and their families."[23] Moreover, many parts of the West were still territories of the United States, anxious to become states. By taking a harder stance against prostitution, gambling, and drinking, local officials knew their image, and chances of statehood would improve substantially.

Gambling had already been restricted somewhat in many parts of the West. For example, some towns allowed gambling only on certain blocks, or limited it to backrooms or screened-off areas. In Sacramento, California, residents passed a law making gambling illegal unless it took place on the second floor of a building.

"Gambling is a thing of the past"

Each time antigambling laws were passed, professional gamblers had moved along, until there were few retreats left. By 1905, only three areas allowed gambling facilities—the territories of Arizona, New Mexico, and Nevada.

Arizona joined the majority in 1907, passing strong antigambling laws. As an editorial in the *Phoenix Gazette* explained, "Gambling is a thing of the past in Phoenix, and the man who looks to the whims of the Goddess of Chance for his livelihood has folded his tent and . . . silently stolen away."[24]

Many Arizona residents were elated, but others felt that the absence of gambling made for a more boring life. Complained one young man, "This place is dead now. Every man, woman, and beast goes to bed at eight o'clock. Sleeping has become one of our principal industries."[25]

Eager for statehood, many territories in the West either banned gambling altogether or restricted where it could take place.

"If you are properly armed with the high sign"

Less than a year later, New Mexico followed Arizona's antigambling lead, leaving only Nevada for legal casinos and other aboveboard gambling activities. But even then pressure from citizens was strong, and finally, in 1909, Nevada enacted similar laws.

The passing of legal gambling in Nevada occurred at midnight, September 30, 1910. Those casinos that had not already closed were jammed with people—some of whom had never seen the inside of a gambling house. Standing shoulder to shoulder at dice and roulette tables, they clamored to make one last bet.

In a move that generated great criticism, Nevada reinstated legal gambling in 1931.

Many assumed that gambling was all but dead, but it did not take long for a few illegal casinos to sprout up secretly around the state. Although the number of gamblers had dwindled, it was still possible for a determined gambler to find a game to wager on. One needed only an "in" with someone—or at least the secret password, as one local newspaper explained: "If you are properly armed with the high sign and the counter sign, and the address, it is said that there is a place in town where the roulette wheel spins nightly."[26]

"Nevada is tired of . . . virtue"

Nevada was the last to ban legal gambling and the first to reinstate it. In 1931 the nation was in the throes of the Great Depression, and Nevada was harder hit than most states. On the verge of bankruptcy, Nevada sorely missed the influx of money and taxes that gambling had once provided. Towns once bustling with activity around the casinos were now almost deserted.

The passage of laws that once again allowed casino gambling in Nevada was big news around the country. Many states were openly critical; people who had worked hard to show that gambling was a waste of time or morally wrong now felt that their efforts had been undermined by Nevada's greed for "easy" money. One newspaper, Alabama's *Montgomery Advertiser*, ran a sarcastic editorial that declared, "Nevada is tired of cactus, alkali wastes, a sparse population, hard times, and virtue."[27]

The rise of "the meadows"

It was at this time that Las Vegas, the center of the gambling world, really came into its own. Before the 1930s, the city whose name means "the meadows" was a hot, dry little town in the middle of the desert, unremarkable except that it was a railroad stop. Little did anyone suspect how radically it would change over the next twenty years.

In the 1930s, one of President Franklin D. Roosevelt's New Deal construction projects, the mammoth Boulder Dam (later renamed Hoover Dam) began in nearby Boulder City. Thousands of workers were involved in the project and on the weekends they were eager to relax. Because Boulder City was a government town, gambling was illegal. And because this was during Prohibition, when a federal law made the sale and consumption of alcohol illegal, no liquor was to be served or purchased in Boulder City either.

A few miles to the northwest, however, Las Vegas could provide everything the workers could possibly want. Bootlegged liquor (illegally made and sold) was easy to find, prostitution was legal, and, best of all, there were gambling houses. Business in Las Vegas couldn't have been better, and word spread throughout the nation that the little desert city was on the move.

The coming of the mob

Not surprisingly, the Las Vegas business boom drew the attention of organized crime as well. Mobsters had been involved in much of the illegal gambling around the country, such as setting up numbers rackets (a type of illegal lottery), bookmaking on horse and dog races, and casinos in New York, Chicago, and Detroit.

Having been squeezed out of some of these places by local law enforcement, these criminals were more than happy to come to Las Vegas, a place where almost everything was legal. Ironically, it was organized crime that was responsible during the next quarter-century for turning the thriving Las Vegas of the 1930s into the glittering gambling capital of the world.

"Bugsy" Siegel

This evolution actually began with one man, a violent underworld boss from Los Angeles named Benjamin "Bugsy" Siegel. A handsome man, Siegel prided himself on his impeccable taste in fashion—from silk shirts and Italian shoes to monogrammed boxer shorts. He came to Las Vegas in the mid-1940s on business, and was mildly impressed by what he saw. He was convinced, however, that in the hands of a man with vision, the city could become something extraordinary.

The secret, he felt, was to attract the high rollers—the kind of gamblers who would think nothing of betting $10,000 on

The evolution of Las Vegas began with mob boss Benjamin "Bugsy" Siegel, who believed Las Vegas could become something extraordinary.

a hand of poker or a roll of the roulette wheel. To lure the high rollers, Las Vegas needed beautiful hotels and lavish casinos—in Siegel's own words, "something to really make Las Vegas get off its ass."[28]

Siegel built the Flamingo Hotel and Casino, a complex quite unlike anything Las Vegas had seen before. The Flamingo must have been striking in 1946, a showplace in every way, its exterior studded with thousands of little lights in bubbly pink neon. In addition to seventy-seven plush hotel rooms, the sprawling grounds included a golf course, squash

Built by Siegel in 1946, the Flamingo Hotel and Casino was a showplace unlike anything Las Vegas had seen before.

and handball courts, a shooting range, a gym, a stable, boutiques, and a vast casino.

New ideas and a violent end

Siegel built his own accommodations in the Flamingo, too. His rooms were equipped with bulletproof windows, and he

had a secret tunnel leading to an underground garage, where a driver and getaway car were on call twenty-four hours a day.

The Flamingo was not immediately successful, however, which made Siegel's partners nervous—after all, they'd put up nearly $6 million of mob money to pay for the hotel, which stood half-empty. Siegel had another idea, however, that proved to be the core of Las Vegas's success.

He decided to change the focus from the high rollers to the masses. He offered cut-rate rooms and inexpensive food to attract the average citizen. The strategy was to get them to the gambling tables, from which most of his profits would come. As an afterthought, he began flying in movie stars and entertainers from nearby Hollywood to put on nightly shows. Within weeks, the Flamingo was a hot property.

Siegel did not get to enjoy his achievement for long. He was gunned down in what was undoubtedly a gangland-style hit. The motives were unclear; some thought he had skimmed money from his partners, while others claimed he was killed because he had repeatedly beaten his girlfriend, a young woman with ties to the Chicago mob.

An underworld haven

The void Siegel left was filled quickly by other underworld crime figures, who came to Las Vegas with suitcases filled with cash made from various illegal activities. With the end of Prohibition in 1933, the exorbitant profit margins that had accompanied bootlegging had shrunk—one more reason the underworld was looking for another big moneymaker. Casinos seemed a good choice.

Taking their cues from the Flamingo, these men built their own now-legendary hotel-casino complexes in Las Vegas—the Desert Inn, the Thunderbird, the Stardust, and the Tropicana. As Siegel had done, the new owners wooed the average citizen rather than the high rollers. They made the experience affordable, writes one historian, by being "willing to lose money themselves on all the cheap food, beverages, lodging, and entertainment that enticed gamblers into the clubs, because those losses were more than offset by the huge profits gleaned at the gambling tables."[29]

Soon after Siegel's death, numerous hotel casinos modeled after the Flamingo were built, making Las Vegas the gambling capital of the United States.

Lots of profits

The strategy paid off in a big way. First of all, the casino complexes did an enormous amount of business; it is estimated that in the early 1950s they took in about $6 million per year. The gambling tables accounted for most of the profits, since slot machines, roulette, and blackjack games clearly favored the house over any gambler. And since the casinos never closed—they shut down for thirty seconds at the stroke of midnight each New Year's Eve—the money was rolling in.

The large flow of cash benefited the criminal owners in other ways, too. It allowed them to funnel money they were making on illegal activities into their casinos, thereby creating a money-laundering haven. Millions of dollars from drug sales, pornography, and prostitution could be counted as profits in the busy casinos, and would be untraceable by the FBI and other law enforcement agencies.

Not every casino at the time was owned and operated by organized crime; some were legitimate businesses. However, historians agree that without the great amounts of mob money in the 1930s, 1940s, and 1950s, much of Las Vegas would not have existed.

Out of Nevada

Of all the states in the Union, Nevada was the unquestioned capital of American gambling. In fact, Las Vegas was synonymous with gambling—that is, until 1976, when the New Jersey legislature voted to permit gambling in the coastal resort of Atlantic City.

It was a little place, only about the size of New York's Central Park, with a population of thirty-eight thousand. But Atlantic City had a prime location—right on the seaside, with easy proximity to the large New York City population. It had once been a vacation spot for eastern seaboard residents, with inexpensive little shops and eateries. Its history had a dark side, too; during Prohibition it was a center of rum smuggling, and mob bosses like Lucky Luciano and Al Capone were known to schedule meetings there.

The underworld influence remained long after the demise of those gangsters. Local politics had a reputation of being corrupt, and the city fell into decay. Most of the little stores and restaurants were boarded up, and it wasn't considered safe to be in Atlantic City at night.

As one expert notes, "By early 1970, the city had reached its terminal stage of urban decay. . . . [It had been] transformed into a massive slum, with most businesses closed, and young people had moved out, leaving the rotten remains to the elderly and minorities who couldn't afford to escape."[30]

"It's the only way we know to save the town"

In dire economic straits, Atlantic City legalized casinos in 1976 in a last-ditch effort to revitalize the city.

In the early 1970s, casino gambling was promoted as a "magic bullet" that could save Atlantic City. Las Vegas, it was pointed out, was making millions of dollars from tourism, and it was in the middle of a desert! How much more attractive Atlantic City was, with its beautiful board-

walk on the beach, and convenient to heavily populated neighboring cities. With gambling as a lure, proponents of the idea were sure that Atlantic City could regain its luster.

Many in New Jersey weren't so confident. Some questioned the introduction of gambling into a town already notorious for corruption. Not surprisingly, the first bill to legalize casinos was defeated in the New Jersey legislature. However, in 1976, after a strong promotional campaign waged by outside developers—many, say historians, with ties to organized crime—the motion was passed. Just before the vote, Atlantic City mayor Joseph Lazarow summed up the ambivalence of many state residents: "Look," he shrugged, "it's no big honor to have a gambling city, but it's the only way we know to save the town."[31]

By early 1978 a hotel had been renovated, transformed into Atlantic City's first casino. Owners were optimistic as three hundred thousand people poured into Atlantic City on opening weekend. Anticipating revenues of $100 million in its first year, casino operators were ecstatic when it had raked in $225 million by the end of its first fiscal year. For those who promised the return of prosperity, it seemed like a good start.

The floodgates open

Around the country, other towns in dire economic straits looked at Atlantic City with interest. They read about more casinos being built, and noted the astronomical totals of visitors and the money they spent. Ten years after Atlantic City opened its casino, the floodgates opened.

In 1988 casino gambling was approved in Deadwood, South Dakota, for the same purpose—to revive a dying area. Deadwood was an old mining town that for some years had relied on tourists who wanted to see where frontier marshal-turned-gambler Wild Bill Hickok had been gunned down in the middle of a poker hand. He'd been holding two pair when he died—aces and eights, which afterward became known as the "dead man's hand."

But with the waning of interest in the Wild West, there was little left in Deadwood to interest tourists. A casino or two seemed a good solution. Nothing elaborate like Las Vegas,

Seeking a way to bring in more tourists and revenue, Deadwood, South Dakota, legalized casinos in 1988.

said the townspeople, just a saloon or two, and some slot machines.

A host of states followed—Illinois, Iowa, and Louisiana, among others. Those states that were squeamish about allowing casinos to be built within their boundaries approved it on riverboats that could chug up and down the Mississippi River, carrying boatloads of gamblers.

Gambling fever

Gambling fever seemed to have taken hold in the United States in a big way. It seemed that every month or so another change in state laws would permit some form of gambling that had been previously banned. The lottery, for example, returned to New Hampshire in 1963, as a means of boosting that state's economy.

Other states followed New Hampshire's lead—slowly at first, but as federal aid to states was cut during the Reagan administration, dozens of states quickly established their own lotteries. Today, thirty-eight states plus the District of Columbia have organized lotteries, and the sale of those tickets has mushroomed to $335.8 billion per year.

But the most interesting development in the gambling world was the coming of casino gambling to an unlikely setting—the Indian reservation. Those casinos, some of the most elegant in the country, and the money they generate have been the source of a great deal of dissension in the past two decades.

3

Indian Casinos

THE RETURN OF legalized gambling—state lotteries and casinos, especially—has been prompted largely in response to floundering state and local economies. It is not surprising that the various Indian reservations in the United States became interested, too.

After all, reasoned many Indian officials, most reservations have been places of poverty and despair since they were established by the U.S. government. Unemployment is rampant, often as high as 75 percent. The rate of suicide is more than twice the national average, alcoholism seven times more prevalent than in the general population. The incidence of tuberculosis and the infant mortality rate matches those of some of the most abject Third World countries.

Why not?

Conditions worsened considerably in the 1980s because both the Reagan and Bush administrations cut programs that had benefited Indians. Budgets for Housing and Urban Development, the Community Services Administration, and the Economic Development Administration, which had provided much-needed services during President Jimmy Carter's administration, were slashed during the Republican years. "The Reagan cuts devastated tribes," explains Frank Ducheneaux, a member of the House of Representatives Indian Affairs Committee. "Since most have high rates of unemployment and poverty and rely heavily on the government for social services, Indians had to find alternative sources of funding."[32]

Some reservations raised livestock to generate income; others sold handcrafted items such as jewelry and woven baskets. The Pequots of Connecticut depended on two industries, a maple syrup business and a hydroponic greenhouse where they raised lettuce year-round. However, few of these endeavors earned enough money to improve the reservations' situation much.

But the early success of the new casinos around the country intrigued Indian leaders. After all, if a dying economy like that of Deadwood, South Dakota, could be jump-started with a casino and a few slot machines, they wondered, why couldn't the same thing happen to Native Americans?

Not fair?

Many reservations had held bingo nights in states where gambling was legal. Prizes were usually fairly small—between

Many reservations already offered bingo when Indian officials began to consider what other forms of gambling they could offer to increase revenue.

$10 and $100. However, in the early 1980s, some reservations began offering larger prizes to attract more players and thereby raise more money.

In 1979, Miami Seminoles in Florida defied a state law prohibiting bingo prizes of more than $100, and began holding games worth $10,000 in a twelve-hundred-seat bingo hall. The state sued, but a federal appeals court ruled that state regulations did not apply to the Seminoles, who were by law a sovereign nation. A similar situation occurred in California in 1980 with card rooms on the Cabazon reservation near Palm Springs, with a similar result in the courts.

State governments were angry; they felt that not only were Indian reservations defying local laws but off-reservation legal gambling was losing business and clearly unable to compete. Granted, the reservations were considered sovereign nations, but didn't they still have to obey the laws of the states in which they were located?

A ruling and a law

A flurry of Indian gambling halls in other states resulted in more legal challenges. Some were upset because reservations were opening small casinos—a type of gambling that was not legal in the rest of the state. In 1987 these challenges reached the U.S. Supreme Court in two cases; the result was a resounding victory for the reservations.

The Court decided, explains *Washington Monthly* reporter David Segal, "that Indians could operate any form of gambling already permitted by the state—and could do so with their own regulations. In the fourteen states that allowed groups to run highly restricted 'Las Vegas nights' for charity, the door was opened for Indians to start up a full blown casino."[33]

In other words, any activity allowed by a state—even in a very limited version—could be offered by its reservations. If a state allowed special church bingo games once a year, bingo could be offered at any time by the reservations located within that state. It was up to the Indians themselves to establish the amount of the cash prizes, sizes of the games, how often they could be played, and so on.

The following year, Congress passed the Indian Gaming Regulatory Act (IGRA), which approved gambling as "a means of promoting tribal economic development, self-sufficiency, and strong tribal governments." Although it allows cooperation between reservations and state governments on some issues such as keeping organized crime out of the gambling enterprises, it formally recognizes the rights of Indians to conduct their business free of outside control.

Gambling, considered by many Indians to be "the new buffalo," generates a steady source of income that allows reservations to support themselves.

"The new buffalo"

It did not take long for several tribes to take advantage of these new opportunities. More and more reservations looked into the feasibility of opening their own gambling establishments. By 1998, casinos and other gambling houses on Indian reservations had become a $6 billion a year industry. Approximately 284 bingo halls and casinos were owned by 185 tribes throughout the United States.

Each reservation deals with the profits of its casinos in its own way. In southern Minnesota, for example, Dakota communities share the money equally by giving cash payments to each registered member of the tribe—an amount between $2,000 and $5,000 per month. Others set the money aside in trusts, to be used later for projects to benefit the tribe collectively. Some of these projects have included the construction of schools and health centers, improved housing, and sewer systems. On their Wisconsin reservation, the Oneida tribe's profitable bingo hall has pumped enough money back to the reservation to build a $10.5 million hotel and convention complex as well as an environmental testing lab that has won both state and federal contracts.

The gambling business is often referred to by Indians as "the new buffalo." Just as the buffalo was once critical to the Plains Indians' survival—providing food, shelter, and other necessities—gambling has proven to be a steady source of income for some tribes. And no tribe has benefited more from gambling than the Pequots of Connecticut, whose casino is the most successful of them all.

The most successful of them all

The place is Foxwoods Resort Casino, and it opened in February 1992 as a large bingo hall with a small number of gaming tables and no slot machines. At first its owners had no idea how popular it would be. "We didn't really think about having it [open] 24 hours a day," says a senior vice president at Foxwoods. "Well, that changed the day we opened."[34]

The response to the casino—then the only one in New England—was tremendous, and the casino has been expanded several times. Today Foxwoods is the largest casino complex on the planet, its 250,000 square feet dwarfing its next largest competitor, the MGM Grand

Casino in Las Vegas. In all, the complex has cost $650 million and employs approximately 12,000 people.

It was estimated in 1996 that 45,000 customers a day come to Foxwoods, either to play its 4,428 slot machines or to bet on roulette, blackjack, or any number of other table games. Every hour an average of $93,000 is lost at those slots or tables.

The profit totals of Foxwoods are not released, since it is a privately owned company. However, the slot machines alone are reaping unheard-of profits. In July 1999, the slot revenue for the month was just over $700 million. The money seems to simply pour in—making it necessary for tribal officials to make weighty decisions about how to use it.

Investing in the community

Rather than pay large amounts of money to each member of the tribe, Pequot elders have decided to first invest

Foxwoods Resort Casino on the Mashantucket Pequot Indian Reservation in Ledyard, Connecticut, is the largest casino complex in the world.

money in their community. They have built a state-of-the-art fire station for the reservation, as well as a multi-million-dollar community center.

In addition to modernizing their reservation, the Pequots have made significant investments in maintaining their heritage and culture. They contributed $10 million to the Smithsonian Institution's Museum of the American Indian in Washington, D.C., and have built a $130 million museum on their reservation, concentrating on the history of the Eastern Woodland tribes. Best of all, they say, they have purchased land to expand the size of their reservation—from two hundred acres to a little more than five thousand.

Positive responses to reservation gambling

The success of places like Foxwoods and other reservation casinos around the United States has had positive effects on non-Indian businesses, as well. Car rental agencies and charter bus companies, for example, have seen their profits skyrocket since the passage of the IGRA.

"We do a lot of day trip stuff," says one driver from Minnesota. "We have buses that bring people in from various parts of the state to Mystic Lake Casino here—and those people have a ball! They are regular, steady customers—they wouldn't have any other way to get here, since lots of them are seniors. We've probably quadrupled our profits since Mystic opened."[35]

Many state officials are pleased because the casinos are large employers. A decline in unemployment rates means that people have more money to spend, and that creates a more prosperous state economy. The employment numbers are reflected not only in the number of people directly employed by the casino; other companies (such as the charter bus agencies) hire more people as a result of the casino's success. So do nearby restaurants, gas stations, and any other businesses frequented by people traveling to the casino.

In the case of Foxwoods, it is estimated that directly and indirectly the casino is responsible for the jobs of thirty thousand people in the state of Connecticut. This is especially good news for that state, says Labor Department econ-

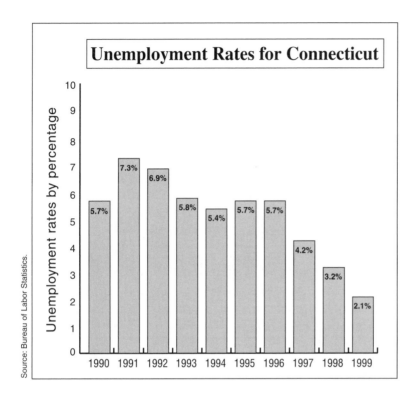

Source: Bureau of Labor Statistics.

omist Lincoln Dyer, because other factors had decreased Connecticut's employment rate in recent years:

> [Foxwoods has] been especially great for the area, that's undoubtedly true. About 1,200 jobs were lost when the naval facility left. We're still trying to match the peak of jobs that the state had in the 1980s, before the recession. But [the area where the casino is] is moving ahead at a faster rate than most of the state.[36]

Not everyone shares the prosperity

There is a difference of opinion, however, on the effect of reservation casinos on nearby businesses. Undoubtedly, some will prosper, but others—especially those that compete with various aspects of a casino—suffer as a result of their proximity to it.

In Oregon, where the Seven Feathers Hotel and Casino opened recently, many nearby say that business has never been worse. One restaurant that used to do more than $25,000 of business per month now has dropped to less than $10,000. The proprietor says people who used to turn off the highway at his exit now go one farther to turn off at the casino exit—and that's the difference in his business.

It makes sense for people to eat at the casino restaurant, he admits, and he knows that he—and others like him—can't compete. And because jobs in a small town are limited, such a development has severe consequences for the community. "In the last year and a half," he shrugs, "[the casino] has put three restaurants out of business. There's nothing but empty storefronts in town."[37]

"We used to be able to see the stars"

Not surprisingly, other gambling venues tend to be critical of the growth of reservation casinos. In California, racetrack and card club owners concede that their establishments seem uninteresting to the gambling public when compared with the super-casinos opening nearby.

Two men watch a horse race on video screens. In California, racetrack owners admit that their establishments seem uninteresting when compared to reservation casinos.

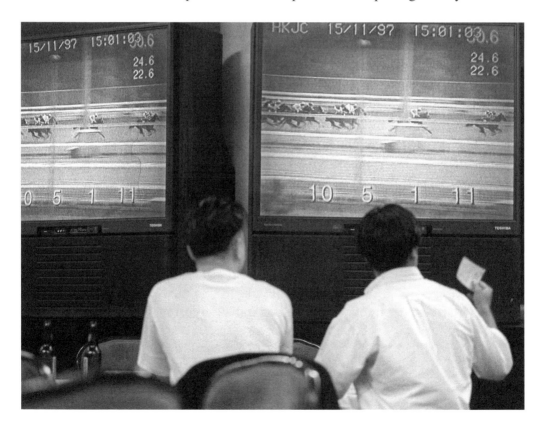

In Los Angeles County, business at established venues has dwindled as casinos have opened in recent years. The gross revenue of the seven card clubs plummeted $26 million in 1997, and were expected to drop further the following year.

Racetrack owners are equally pessimistic. "There's no place in this country where casino gambling has been compatible with horse racing," says one employee. "Horse racing always loses."[38]

Aside from the economic impact of Indian casinos, there have been other, more basic, concerns. For instance, when large-scale gambling begins on a reservation, the quiet rural atmosphere of the surrounding area often changes, which worries many homeowners.

"When we arrived here eleven years ago," says one woman whose home is close to Foxwoods, "there were cows across the street and no street lights. But our road is good and it goes directly to the casino. We have so many taxis go by now, I can hail one at the foot of my driveway. . . . We used to be able to see the stars at night, but it's like when a mall comes with bright lights—you can't see the stars anymore. Damn casino."[39]

The threat of organized crime

Another concern that is frequently voiced is that of the role of organized crime in reservation gambling. The heavy underworld influence had finally been addressed as a serious problem in Las Vegas and Atlantic City by the U.S. government in the 1950s and 1960s, and casino operations are now closely watched by the Internal Revenue Service and the FBI. State gaming boards constantly police the gambling industry within their borders.

However, because of their sovereign status, Indian reservations are not required to submit to the same scrutiny. Names of organized crime figures that are known to casino operators in Nevada and Atlantic City, for example, are not always familiar to Indian casino bosses—and that could cause serious problems.

Donald Trump, New York developer and casino owner, who has long criticized the IGRA as being preferential to Indians, charged in 1993 that reservation gambling is often corrupt. "A lot of the reservations are being, at least to a certain extent, run by organized crime," he maintained. "There's no protection. It's become a joke."[40]

Exaggerated statements

Experts say that Trump's statements are exaggerated. In some instances, people with ties to organized crime have attempted to infiltrate reservation casinos, and most of these problems came in the first year or two of legalized Indian casinos. Because of their sovereign status, reservations had a more difficult time getting loans to build their casino complexes because they possessed no collateral. Since their land is considered a "perpetual trust" (meaning that it can never be taken away), there is nothing a bank can foreclose on if the loan is not repaid.

This meant that some reservations were more vulnerable to lenders with shady associates, who were often only too eager to lend the millions needed to build casinos. Though not frequent, these problems alarmed both reservation officials and law enforcement agencies. Efforts to keep organized crime out of the Indian casinos led to the establishment of the National Indian Gaming Commission in 1993. The NIGC works with the Department of Justice and the Bureau of Indian Affairs to ensure that anyone associated with reservation casinos undergoes thorough background checks.

Law enforcement officials say now that, while it is impossible to guarantee that reservation casinos are completely free of individuals with such ties, they are no more susceptible today than any other casino. "Every new casino market, Indian and non-Indian," says gambling expert Timothy O'Brien, "has drawn old gangsters out of the woodwork."[41]

Tribal officials have said that charges like Trump's are rooted in jealousy and prejudice rather than fact. They say that organized crime is almost nonexistent today, even though critics of the IGRA continue to demean their casinos. "There's no organized crime, reorganized crime, or dis-

organized crime on Indian reservations," says one NIGC official. "What critics of Indian gaming are really afraid of is organized Indians."[42]

More personal costs

While the threat of organized crime worries some, many issues related to gambling concern tribal officials more. One of the most important has been the controversy over the fundamental appropriateness of gambling.

Donald Trump, seen here in front of his casino in Atlantic City, has long criticized the IGRA as being preferential to Indians.

Many Indians say that casinos and the activity they represent go against the Indian way of life. Gambling, they insist, is not an honorable, hardworking way to make a living, nor is it right to live off the losses of gamblers by working in a casino. They say also that gambling puts an unhealthy emphasis on making money and accumulating material things—goals that traditional Indian cultures have taught their people to avoid.

"Our people are taught to work the honest way," says one elder of the Hopi tribe of Arizona who has opposed the opening of a casino on his reservation. "We believe that we are the last to hold a strong and complete tradition, and that if we fail, it will be the end of Native American traditions in this country."[43]

But other tribal members disagree, repeating that gambling is the Indians' "new buffalo." Since so many other attempts at making money on the reservations have failed, they say, why not start a business that is almost a guaranteed money-maker? The strong differences of opinion between the two sides have caused anger and, in one tragic situation, a war. Many Indians say that this war, in which Indians fought against Indians at a reservation called Akwesasne, shows how dangerous the issue of reservation gaming can be.

Akwesasne

The trouble began in the late 1980s, on a twenty-eight-thousand-acre reservation that sprawls over the U.S.-Canada border near the St. Lawrence River. More than many reservations, Akwesasne has had a great deal of trouble with unemployment and poverty. With three rivers and great expanses of land, it would seem to be a perfect place to raise livestock and crops. However, three nearby industrial plants—Reynolds, Alcoa, and General Motors—have made Akwesasne one of the most polluted sites in the United States. Writes one researcher:

> Agriculture, which made the Mohawks self-sufficient, was slowly destroyed. Fluoride caused cows to lose their teeth. The PCBs seeping into the groundwater and soil made anything grown at Akwesasne suspect. The fish that survive in

the Saint Lawrence are no longer edible, so laden is the river with heavy metals. The marshes, once productive hunting and trapping grounds, were flooded by the completion, in 1959, of the St. Lawrence Seaway.[44]

Another problem is competition for reservation leadership. Akwesasne is home to the Mohawk nation, but partly because it straddles two countries (as well as a state and two provinces), several groups have been vying for power.

Many Indians who believe in their traditions are trying to keep their heritage alive; they argue that gambling goes against the Indian way of life.

The result is a number of councils, each claiming to be the true officials of the reservation. New York State recognizes one council as the reservation leaders, but another has been recognized by the Quebec provincial government and another by the Canadian federal government. Consensus was impossible.

When legalized gambling became an option for reservations in the early 1980s, some people at Akwesasne were eager to have a casino. One council built a large bingo palace. By 1989 six more gambling houses had followed, but although business was booming, many on the reservation were angry.

Bloodshed on the reservation

Some of the councils who were more conservative about Indian ways spoke out against the casinos. They were antigambling, and called themselves the Antis. They pleaded with the state of New York and the federal government to close the casinos, which they said were built illegally because they had not been approved by the true reservation government.

The progambling groups were known on the reservation as the Warriors. They were infuriated by the Antis' actions, and their anger boiled over into violence. Many on the reservation scrambled to take sides, and arson, drive-by shootings, and death threats to council elders ensued. Hoping to prevent customers from driving to the casinos, the Antis began a routine of putting up roadblocks on the highway. Eventually, in May 1990, a full-scale gun battle erupted between the two sides.

So many shots were fired, says one account, that "Vietnam vets working at the U.S. Customs checkpoint on the international bridge across the St. Lawrence listened and thought they were back in the DMZ [Demilitarized Zone]."[45] When the shooting stopped, two men were dead and the Antis had to flee the reservation for their lives. The Mohawk people, who had weathered so much adversity over the centuries, had been irreparably fragmented.

Other problems

Even when a reservation agrees to build a bingo hall or casino, issues remain. Counselors and health-care workers say that the sudden influx of cash into a community that was very needy can lead to bad spending choices. "When you have a community of people not used to the luxury of a steady income and large sums of money, you create some distortions of what wealth is and how to use it,"[46] says one health-services expert who works with residents of an Arizona reservation. Some reservation residents have used the large cash payments to buy luxury items such as jewelry or sports cars. Some take huge somes of money to the casinos and gamble it away. One counselor reported that an 18-year-old bought so many televisions, stereos, and other expensive electronic equipment, he had boxes stacked outside because there was no room left inside the house.

Money alone is not a cure-all, say experts, and without some serious planning by tribal officials, it can lead to problems among those who are more vulnerable. "Stories began to surface about severe abuses," writes one Native American of a nearby reservation with a new casino. "Crack. Cocaine. The effects—especially among the younger members of the community—of having no financial need or incentive to work."[47]

No magic bullet

Even more worrisome for Indian leaders is the possibility that the American majority will begin to stereotype Indians as wealthy and undeserving of economic and developmental assistance. The success of places like Mystic Lake in Minnesota and Foxwoods in Connecticut has brought a great deal of money to those reservations. However, the idea that gambling is the magic cure-all that will somehow make all Indians rich is simply not true.

Gambling facilities have been opened by fewer than 20 percent of the U.S. tribes. Most of those casinos or bingo halls generate a small fraction of the profits of a Foxwoods, either because their budgets are smaller or because of state restrictions on gambling.

Many tribes could not even consider opening a casino because of their isolation. For instance, more than eighty-five thousand Native Americans live in Alaska, where 80 percent of the villages can't be reached by roads; no casino could benefit them. Nor could one help Navajos in remote Arizona deserts.

"We should applaud those that have found routes out of poverty through casinos or other means," insists Ben Nighthorse Campbell, a senator from Colorado. "But just because a small percentage of tribes can make it through gambling, private donors and public agencies should not abandon the less fortunate reservations."[48]

4

Is Gambling a Good Bet?

WITH GAMBLING NOT only legal but socially acceptable in the United States, far more people participate today. According to the casino industry, the number of American households visiting casinos doubled between 1990 and 1993—and the rate has continued to climb every year since then.

This dramatic increase in participation has prompted a great deal of recent debate about gambling. People question whether the gambling industry is a benefit to the community, as it claims to be. Others examine the social and economic advantages of casinos and lotteries, and wonder if the United States is better off as a gambling nation.

White tigers, pirate battles, and volcanoes

Nowhere is the concept of a "gambling nation" better demonstrated than in Las Vegas. No longer does the city hold a monopoly on casino action; people do not have to travel across the country to the Nevada desert to play slot machines and blackjack. There are scores of brightly lit, energy-packed casinos much closer to home, and many of them offer big-name entertainment, too. Therefore, to continue to exist, Las Vegas has had to change with the times.

The new casinos in Las Vegas have adopted the image of fantasy resorts—marvelous places that must be seen to be believed. As one writer explains, "[The owners' aim] is to bedazzle customers, creating must-see attractions that will

In order to compete with casinos in other parts of the country, resort owners in Las Vegas have created establishments that are "must-see" attractions.

draw millions of new players and keep the old ones coming back."[49] The Mirage, for example, has the only man-made volcano in the world. Standing fifty-four feet high, it spews smoke and fire on cue, every fifteen minutes. In addition to state-of-the-art gambling facilities, the $630 million resort features dolphins frolicking in a seaquarium and rare white tigers prowling in a special grotto near the casino entrance.

Theme parks are big. The Circus-Circus Excalibur features a huge theme park set in King Arthur's time. A real jousting pit is surrounded by a dinner theater, so customers can watch mounted knights battle. A $1 billion Wizard of Oz park attracts visitors to the MGM complex.

"Disneyland with dice"

The hope of these casinos is that parents will view a gambling trip as a family activity. In most of the new complexes, there are plenty of activities to lure children and occupy them while their parents slip off to the roulette tables.

Video arcades, strolling cartoon characters, and large amusement parks provide a kid-friendly environment—something Las Vegas has not had in the past. Casino owners say that parents who know that their kids are safe and happy are more relaxed about gambling—and feel less guilt. Says one observer, "The new Vegas wants to be Disneyland with dice."[50]

"I think it's a great idea," says Ray, who with his wife, Penny, just returned from a ten-day stay in Las Vegas with their two daughters. "We'd always talked about going—we should have done it before we had kids, you know? Because then you get busy, and you just don't want to think about the hassle. And here we are now, with two girls, and it's even more appealing than we thought.

"It was actually my oldest daughter that suggested it—she'd heard about the casinos with the Oz theme, and the one with the pirate ships, and the three-story pyramid from a friend. So we thought about it, and we decided, why not? The kids swam, rode the rides, went to the arcade. They had a ball. Penny and I gambled, and we had fun. Oh, yeah, we're going back next year!"[51]

High rollers

This "bring the family" attitude does not mean that Las Vegas casinos are not

The water ride in MGM Grand's theme park in Las Vegas is just one attraction meant to appeal to the whole family.

interested in luring the big gamblers, the high rollers who spend more on a single turn of the roulette wheel or a hand of baccarat than many people earn in a year. The high rollers are still highly sought-after—mostly because they are a great source of revenue for the casinos.

These gamblers can win big—sometimes a million or more in an evening. But they can turn around and lose that million or more the very next day. A high roller is given a generous line of credit by the casino, since by doing so, the establishment increases the chances that he or she will stay longer, and thus lose more money. But there are other perks offered by casinos that are serious about luring high rollers, perks that the average gambler can only dream about.

High rollers are given complimentary meals and free rooms at the hotel for as long as they wish (or until they stop gambling). A casino will almost always pick up the tab for high rollers' airfare, as well. They are assigned a personal host, whose job is to make sure the guest is given red-carpet treatment, even down to a favorite chef who is on call twenty-four hours a day!

Skewed games

But while many casinos actively court the high rollers, it is still the average, middle-income gamblers that provide the lion's share of their profits. Whether in Las Vegas, Atlantic City, or on an Indian reservation, successful casinos have learned a thing or two about how to make the most money from each customer. Most gamblers are not aware of these methods, a fact many critics of gambling like to point out.

The most important aim of any casino, say experts, is to keep the customer sitting at the gambling table as long as possible. The longer he continues playing, the more money he will lose. Explains the president of one Atlantic City casino, "Our goal is not to get more out of a customer in three hours, but to get him to stay for four hours."[52]

This tactic works, of course, because all casino games are designed to give the edge, or advantage in odds, to the house. Whether the game is a slot machine, a blackjack game, or a spin of the roulette wheel, the casino will win most of the time.

Most of the money that circulates throughout a casino will end up staying there.

Tricks of the trade

To keep people in their establishments as long as possible, casinos prefer that their customers not be reminded how much time is passing. Noting, for instance, that the afternoon sun has set might alert a customer to the fact that she has been there for hours longer than she planned to stay. Thus, one would be hard pressed to find a clock or a window in any casino.

Studies have also shown that certain colors seem to increase a player's response to slot machines. Dark, rich colors

Bright lights and certain colors have been found to increase a player's interest in slot machines.

such as blue, black, and purple are especially pleasing to gamblers, so new machines in those colors are replacing ones in white, yellow, or silver. Lighting, too, has been correlated to how long people will sit at a gaming table—when light reflects into their eyes, they tend to become tired more quickly. That's why many casinos are now changing their lighting fixtures to illuminate the table, not the players.

At least three large Las Vegas casinos have been experimenting with certain scents. Some studies have indicated that a certain spray circulating in the casino's air may actually influence bettors to stay longer. Sounds, too, can be "triggers" for gamblers. That's why the payoff of quarters that tumbles out of a winning slot machine falls into a purposely metallic tray—known in casinos as the "loud bowl." Says one researcher, "A noisy payout is essential, for it reminds the player, and all those around her, that money does, in fact, talk."[53]

Money, money, money

The tricks of the trade are not limited to lighting and atmosphere. Some of the most effective practices are those that make it easier for gamblers and their money to part company. There is no need to budget lots of extra cash for food and drink, for example; most casinos have circulating waitresses with free drinks and offer ridiculously inexpensive all-you-can-eat buffets.

An important first order of business in a casino is to get the customer to exchange as much cash as possible for chips. Once dollars are converted into multicolored chips, they don't have as much importance to the gambler. Explains one chief of operations at a Las Vegas casino, "If you give a guy a $100 bill, he looks at it like a round of golf, a golf cart, two beers and a hot dog. But if you give him chips, it's just betting units and it loses its value."[54]

It's not even necessary to get up from the gaming table to exchange cash for more chips. Casino workers regularly circulate to provide that service. And when giving a customer chips, workers are instructed to give lower denominations, which will be spent more readily. A $25 chip, on the other hand, might be pocketed and saved, and turned in for cash at the end of the night.

Do gamblers ever win?

Because the odds favor the house in casino games, over the long stretch, the casino will always win, even though there are certainly occasional big winners and frequent small ones. However, there is one game at which it is possible to increase one's odds to a slight advantage over the house—blackjack.

Unlike games like roulette and slot machines, blackjack (or 21, as it is often called) involves some skill. In 1962 a mathematician named Ed Thorp wrote a book called *Beat the Dealer*, in which he showed how a clever card player can increase those odds. The book's methods have been refined and reworked by others over the years, but the idea is basically the same: Keep track of the cards that have been played so that you can more accurately predict what cards are left in the deck.

Casinos keep their patrons at gaming tables longer by offering free drinks and providing roving employees who will exchange cash for more chips.

People who can keep a mental running tally of the cards that have been played—especially the aces, face cards, and tens—are known as card counters. They are quick to explain that they cannot win all the time counting cards. Many, says expert Timothy O'Brien, "have to endure numbing losing streaks, which will crush them if their bankrolls aren't big enough."[55] It is an advantage that will pay out only over time.

The enemy of casinos

Not surprisingly, casino operators consider card counters their worst enemies. Although judges have ruled in various lawsuits that counting cards is not cheating, many casinos still claim the right to throw out an individual they suspect of card counting. Stories abound of people who have been permanently banned from casinos.

Some of the best card counters use disguises, since all casinos keep books with photographs of known counters. Others band with other counters into groups and pool their winnings. But the casinos have fought back, using state-of-the-art technology to watch customers who seem to be winning consistently.

The odds of going broke in America will be increasing.

Reprinted by permission of Ed Gamble.

Special cameras above the blackjack tables are used to monitor a suspected counter's cards, and how he plays them. The results are fed into a computer with a database of more than two dozen known card-counting methods. If the computer indicates that one of them is in use, the customer is ordered to leave the casino.

A card counter who is willing to travel extensively can make upwards of $250,000 a year. Most, however, are happy to walk away with one-quarter of that. Part of the fun, they acknowledge, is beating the casino at its own game—evening the odds, so to speak. Even so, the activity has its disadvantages.

"Playing blackjack is really a very lonely way to make a living," admits one counter. "In any normal occupation, as you get better at what you do, you advance, you receive a little recognition. It's not like that with cards. The better you become, the more vilified you are—and the more you have to conceal who you are."[56]

"A little spoonful of hope"

Critics of gambling often point to the subtle manipulations of casinos, saying that the public is almost always encouraged to overbet and to stay too long. To make matters worse, they say, gamblers—whether playing casino games or buying lottery tickets—are almost always losers, while the casinos or the state get richer. And when someone, such as a card counter, develops a method of winning back some of the public's money, he is threatened and barred from the casino.

However, many gamblers insist that they are not victims, and that they feel that gambling is not harmful to them as individuals. They say that gambling is risk taking, something that they are not always able to do in other aspects of their lives. "Casino gambling is risk taking in its purest form," says one. "The participants willingly and deliberately get involved, knowing the chances are not in their favor. No one has to do it."[57] Others say that the games provide a glimmer of hope (though admittedly small) of striking it rich with one roll of the dice or a one-dollar lottery ticket. The activity, says one gambling advocate, gives people "a little spoonful of hope, which, like honey, is pleasing while it lasts."[58]

Many people defend gambling as a free choice and bristle at the prospect of government taking away that freedom. "I have received letters from some people who are very emotional," says one state lottery official. "They say, 'Who is the state to tell me how I spend my income? . . . And if I want to spend my money on a lottery ticket versus someone spending ten or twenty thousand dollars on a country club membership, that's my privilege and that's my right.'"[59]

Cost to society?

But while individual gamblers may understand the one-sided games they are playing, and defend their right to spend their money as they please, the same is not always true for society as a whole. Some of the harshest critics of gambling say that the track record of the industry has already established it as harmful. One of the biggest complaints about gambling is that it has not delivered on the financial promises it has made to states and local communities.

Atlantic City, for example, legalized gambling with the understanding that it would be, in the words of the New Jersey Casino Controls Act, "a unique tool of urban development" that would "facilitate the redevelopment of existing blighted areas, and the refurbishing and expansion of existing hotel, convention, tourist, and entertainment facilities."[60]

However, gambling's effect on Atlantic City has been profoundly negative, say many observers. Instead of thriving, over one-third of existing retail businesses have closed. Any restaurant, bar, or shop that might have been a rival to the casino complexes simply couldn't compete. The town has become two towns—the glittering casinos on one side, and the boarded-up, glass-littered former business district on the other. "Atlantic City used to be a slum by the sea," observes law professor I. Nelson Rose. "Now it's a slum by the sea with casinos."[61] The casinos, of course, have done well, and some of their revenue has come back to the city in the form of taxes; however, some have criticized city leaders for their priorities in spending. When the $14.5 million Sandcastle

Stadium was built, critics commented that the last thing Atlantic City needed was an expensive new sports facility.

"Just look at this place," says one community leader. "It's decimated. . . . There's a skill shortage here. People don't have a work ethic or a desire to work. We need job training programs, not a minor league baseball stadium."[62]

Despite the success of the casinos, gambling in Atlantic City has not rejuvenated the city as expected.

Surprises in Deadwood

Deadwood, South Dakota, has had a similar experience. Gambling was only a hook to get tourists back to the area, many residents thought. Once in Deadwood, people would be charmed by the Black Hills and the local color. However, "a few little casinos" multiplied to eighty by 1996, with twenty-five thousand slot machines.

The town of eighteen hundred residents had other unpleasant surprises. There were nine stores in downtown Deadwood before the casinos came; within a year all were gone. The little cafe where locals dropped in to chat with neighbors couldn't afford to stay, since property taxes rose so high. Residents who were once employed locally now find themselves driving long distances to other towns, or underemployed working in a casino. Crime—especially theft and forgery—has increased three-fold.

While many residents are furious over the changes gambling has made in their town, others say that some good has come of it. There is more tax revenue for city projects, for education, and the revitalization of some of the historic buildings in Deadwood. But others feel that the community has been permanently changed for the worse.

Lottery promises

Like other forms of gambling, state lotteries, while bringing in gigantic profits, are increasingly under criticism for the way they use that money. Many states claim that the money goes for education; however, it is not necessarily used as *additional* funding, to complement what is collected for education through taxes. Quite often, it simply replaces tax money—a fact most voters aren't aware of.

St. Mary's College did a study of educational budgets in all fifty states and found that those states whose education money comes from lotteries give less to education than states that do not have lotteries. Part of the reason is that enrollments are rising, so there is more of a demand for funds—yet the sales of lottery tickets are not rising. In addition, the increasing administrative costs of running a lottery mean that there is less money earned by the state.

So rather than augment the budget, add a new program to state schools, or purchase musical instruments or physical education equipment, the money is being spent just as tax money was spent—except in lesser amounts.

"We've been hurt by our lottery," says a spokesman for the Florida Education Association. "The state has simply replaced general revenues with lottery money—at a time when enrollments are increasing. It's a big shell game."[63]

Dangerous practice

The increasing dependence of communities on gambling revenue alarms many economists. They worry lest lottery or casino revenues become a permanent line item in state budgets. What happens when gambling reaches a saturation point in the United States, and it loses its allure? What will happen to the state education budgets then?

Gambling is not a "try it and see what happens" kind of experiment; once a community or state says "yes" to gambling, it becomes committed to gambling. "Once the casino opens and the dice begin to roll," says one casino expert, "gambling creates an instant constituency. People depend on it for jobs. Governments depend on it for revenues."[64]

Gambling and crime

Another aspect of gambling that worries many people is its connection to rising crime rates. Atlantic City, for example, went from fiftieth in the nation in per capita crime to first, within three years of the opening of the first casino there. Street crime is rampant there, with assaults and armed robberies up significantly. One recent study done by Rutgers University found that prostitution in Atlantic City has become so widespread that law enforcement felt it would be impossible to curtail, and recommended legalizing it instead.

As for the role of organized crime in gambling today, experts agree that such criminals are no longer the casino owners and operators. The increased vigilance of the FBI and the Internal Revenue Service makes it more difficult for organized crime to use gambling establishments for money laundering and other illegal acts.

However, they also agree that there is still a great deal of organized crime indirectly connected with gambling. "The

Critics argue that gambling is not healthy for society because it generates crime, a dependency on the revenue, and a growing number of addicts.

godfathers and the wise guys did not just disappear from the casinos when Wall Street arrived," reports one researcher. "Like many founders leaving a business, they were smart enough to figure out ways to continue getting paid."[65]

Firms with connections to such criminals arrange some gambling junkets and group tours, provide limos and bus transportation, and book entertainment in the casinos' show rooms. The mob is also involved in the distribution of illegal slot machines, for which it takes a cut of the profits. And though organized crime is not a visible presence in legalized gambling, it is still very active in the illegal side of it. It continues to operate under-the-counter sports betting and numbers running, and even owns illegal casinos in most major cities in the United States.

One FBI official feels that widespread opportunities for legal gambling have increased the numbers of new gamblers. The more gamblers, the more business for illegal operations. "Gambling generates new gambling," he says. "The more accepted it becomes, the more all forms of gambling benefit."[66]

But while crime and economic troubles are worrisome, the aspect of gambling that most concerns its critics is the growing number of problem gamblers—those whose compulsions and bad choices threaten not only themselves and their families, but the health of society.

5

When Gambling Becomes a Problem

THE ASPECT OF gambling that has caused the most recent controversy is the question "Who is doing the gambling?" Researchers have conducted demographic studies to determine what sort of people gamble most frequently, and their findings are troublesome to both critics and supporters of gambling in the United States.

Who gambles?

One of the most interesting findings of the studies is that most gambling is being done by a very small part of the population. In a 1998 study of lottery ticket sales, for example, Duke University professors Charles Clotfelter and Phillip Cook found that although a wide variety of people buy lottery tickets, 5 percent of lottery players actually account for 51 percent of the ticket sales.

They also discovered that the most frequent players are households that earn less than $10,000 a year. Says Cook, "The sense that everybody plays and it's a broad-based participation is absolutely true, but the people who are important in terms of revenue are the small percentage paying $3,500 a year or more."[67] Without those players, lottery ticket sales for 1997 would have dropped from $36 billion to $7.4 billion.

Another study in Nebraska found that people at or below the poverty line spend an average of 7 percent of their income on lottery tickets or casino gambling. Those in middle or upper brackets spend 2 or 3 percent. In Illinois, researchers learned that some of the poorest suburbs of Chicago have the most gambling; in one town the average monthly gambling expenditure was $100 per month.

"This could be your ticket out"

Many critics of gambling blame the gambling industry; they feel that the poor and minorities are being unfairly targeted by enticing gambling advertisements. They say that people in desperate life circumstances lack the skills to get a good job, and see the lottery as an easy way to get rich. Billboards advertising the Illinois lottery in some of the poorest, most crime-ridden neighborhoods of Chicago read, "This could be your ticket out."[68]

Many low-income people are also undereducated and frequently are not aware of how tiny the chance of actually hitting the jackpot really is. They are more easily impressed

than more highly educated people by ads such as one for the Connecticut state lottery, which shows a retiree fishing on a lake. He laughs as he tells the camera, "I never planned for the future. I never saved. I never did anything they told me to. What I did was play the Connecticut lotto game and I won umpteen million dollars and here I am!"[69]

However, lottery officials deny that they are unfairly targeting any particular group of Americans. Besides, they say, it is a voluntary game—no one is forced to participate. They also argue that if lotteries cease as a method of making money for the state, money will have to be raised as taxation, and then lottery players will not have a choice about whether they spend that money.

Gambling seniors

Another group of gamblers that is considered at risk is America's senior citizens. According to a recent University of Chicago study, the highest rate of increase in gamblers between 1974 and 1999 was adults sixty-five and over. Like many of the lowest-income gamblers, some seniors look at gambling as a real way to make a lot of money.

"I know several elderly guys who are on a fixed income," says one pastor, "and see the casinos as a source of quick cash. Every month without fail, they take their social security check and go to the riverboats."[70]

However, because eventually gamblers always lose more than they gain, many elderly people quickly get into financial trouble, losing not only their social security checks but their savings, as well. This is particularly devastating to an older person, say experts, because the elderly do not have the option that younger people with a long future have to start over when they lose everything.

"It's a lot more fun than cleaning my house"

Many seniors enjoy the element of risk taking that gambling provides; they are products of the depression, and learned the hard way to be frugal with their money. The opportunity to abandon that attitude—even for an afternoon—is a pleasure.

Levels of Gambling Addiction

LEVEL	SYMPTOM
Preoccupation	Is preoccupied with gambling (e.g., preoccupied with reliving past gambling experiences, handicapping or planning the next venture, or thinking of ways to get money with which to gamble)
Tolerance	Needs to gamble with increasing amounts of money in order to achieve the desired excitement
Withdrawal	Is restless or irritable when attempting to cut down or stop gambling
Escape	Gambles as a way of escaping from problems or relieving dysphoric mood (e.g., feelings of helplessness, guilt, anxiety, or depression)
Chasing	After losing money gambling, often returns another day in order to get even ("chasing one's losses")
Lying	Lies to family members, therapists, or others to conceal the extent of involvement with gambling
Loss of control	Has made repeated unsuccessful efforts to control, cut back, or stop gambling
Illegal acts	Has committed illegal acts (e.g., forgery, fraud, theft, or embezzlement) in order to finance gambling
Risked significant relationship	Has jeopardized or lost a significant relationship, job, or educational or career opportunity because of gambling
Bailout	Has relied on others to provide money to relieve a desperate financial situation caused by gambling

Source: National Opinion Research Center at the University of Chicago, Gemini Research, and The Lewin Group.

The aspect of senior-citizen gambling that is far more troublesome to researchers, however, is what is called "relief escape" gambling. This means that gambling becomes a way to relieve emotions that are painful, such as loneliness, isolation, and boredom—common complaints of older people cut off from family and friends. If gambling is seen as a cure (even a temporary one) for those emotions, it becomes a crutch—and the gambler is close to being addicted.

One woman who comes to Mystic Lake Casino "four or five times every week, if I can get someone to bring me," admits that she gambles because she doesn't have much

According to a recent study, the greatest increase in gamblers between 1974 and 1999 was in the age group sixty-five and older.

else to do. "It's a lot more fun than cleaning my house," she says. "And why should I clean it every day, anyway? It's just me and my dog, and we don't make much of a mess. I think in the old days, you cleaned for family, for friends. I don't have much company.

"So I could clean, or I could wait for my daughter to call. But why? She almost never does. And this is fun, anyway," she laughs. "I feel so good when those quarters come shooting down. So I'm old, so what? Does that mean I can't have fun? Would you rather have me home knitting?"[71]

Some seniors say gambling makes them forget for a few hours that they are old and often in pain. Says one, "When you go [to the casino] you forget your aches and pains. I had a heart attack, I had angioplasty, I had open-heart surgery. . . . And I thought that was the end of my life, that I would never do anything, or enjoy anything. I find in Atlantic City I feel like I'm 18 years old."[72]

The young gamblers

Teens are another group whose numbers as gamblers are growing since the widespread legalization of gambling. For many teens, an excursion to a nearby casino has become almost a rite of passage on one's eighteenth birthday.

"It was like, 'We'll go to the casino and then we'll go to my house for a party,'" says Sara, a high school senior. "It was just assumed we'd go, because everyone goes on their eighteenth. That's just how it is. And everyone gives you five bucks, all your friends, and they watch you gamble. Or in my case—watch me blow it in about ten minutes!"[73]

Though many teens can wager responsibly, many cannot. In fact, say experts, a teenager is twice as likely as any other person to become a problem gambler. Gambling is portrayed in the media as an adult activity, and many teens are in a hurry to appear older. Too, the idea of quick money is tempting to many teens.

"I always needed money," says one teen, who began gambling at age sixteen with a fake ID. "I needed clothes, stuff for my car, and CDs. My parents have a thing about not working during the school year, because they want me to have more time to study and play sports. So I gambled to make money, and sometimes I did."[74]

Gambling's "crack cocaine"

Surveys of young gamblers indicate that their favorite casino activity is the video slot machine. Some psychologists say that teens are far more comfortable than older gamblers with video games, and that is why slots are so alluring. In South Carolina, video poker machines have become so addictive that state officials have nicknamed them "the crack cocaine of gambling."[75]

Teens soon find, however, that money is lost far more often than it is won. Often, the lesson is learned too late, only after great sums of money are spent gambling. One teen gambled away her graduation money, totaling $600. She'd converted it all to change and used it in slot machines.

"I thought the law of averages would mean that eventually I'd get a big hit," she says. "I didn't leave the machine once, not in eight hours. I kept pumping in those quarters, one after another, and pretty soon, I'd cashed in my last $20 and all those quarters were gone. I wanted to kill myself—it dawned on me what I'd done."[76]

Teenagers are finding casinos and gambling irresistible.

Beyond "problem" gambling

Her experience that night taught her a lesson, she says, but she wishes she'd learned it several hundred dollars sooner. Even so, she is convinced she will never gamble in a casino again. Yet for millions of people in the United States, such a loss would not be enough to make them stop. They are compulsive gamblers, people for whom gambling is not entertainment, but an addiction.

Experts say that there are between 6 and 10 million compulsive gamblers in the United States, with another 15 million in the "problem" area, some dangerously close to becoming addicted. As gambling becomes more widespread, analysts predict that the numbers will rise.

Compulsive gambling was officially recognized as a mental disorder by the American Psychiatric Institute in 1980, but it does not have as clear a definition as other forms of addiction. In fact, only 150 gambling counselors are certified throughout the United States, compared with hundreds of thousands of counselors who help address drug and alcohol addictions.

Part of the trouble, say some researchers, is that it is more difficult to spot a gambling addict than a substance abuser.

"It's the hidden disease of the '90s," says Paul Ashe, president of the National Council on Problem Gambling. "You can't see the card tracks on their arms. You can't smell the dice on their breath."[77]

Destroying lives

Although an exact definition is difficult, mental health workers agree on some aspects of compulsive gambling. They know, for example, that compulsive gamblers come from all age, racial, and economic groups. They know that as compulsive gamblers, men outnumbered women 2 to 1 in 1999, but they expect the number of women to grow sizably by 2002.

They agree, too, that compulsive gamblers often destroy their lives and the lives of the people who love them. The vast majority suffer marital breakups and job loss; many also begin to abuse drugs or alcohol. One of five attempts

suicide. The crime rate among compulsive gamblers is staggering—more than 75 percent have committed a felony.

A gambling counselor and her husband create a picture of the financial skid that compulsive gamblers go into:

> Compulsive gamblers will bet until nothing is left: savings, family assets, personal belongings—anything of value that may be pawned, sold, or borrowed against. They will borrow from coworkers, credit unions, family, and friends, but will rarely admit that it is for gambling. They may take personal loans, write bad checks, and ultimately reach and pass the point of bankruptcy. . . . In desperation, compulsive gamblers may panic and often will turn to illegal activities to support their addiction.[78]

Gwen

One who knows this all too well is Gwen, a waitress and a single mother. She has written bad checks and maxed out several credit cards to pay for gambling. She has lied to her boss, telling him she needs a salary increase to pay for an operation for her son. In desperation she has pilfered money from the restaurant's safe, and served a brief jail sentence.

She has suffered bouts of overwhelming depression and guilt, but the only solace she finds are the times she is at the casino, sitting at the poker table. She sometimes gambles for several days straight, she admits, equipped with a toothbrush and a cash card in her purse.

"A lot of people think gambling is harmless," she says. "They don't know it can make you steal, it can make you commit illegal acts. . . . They don't know this is a deadly disease that can kill you."[79]

Gwen regrets much about her addiction to gambling, but no part of it is as agonizing to her as the hurt she's caused her son. She recalls one gambling binge the day of his tenth birthday. She went to buy party supplies, with the best of intentions; she ended up in the casino instead.

Though her family paged her and her son begged her to come home, she stayed there, trying to win back the $2,000 she'd lost earlier in the day. When she finally arrived home, the little boy was huddled in a corner, waiting. "Mom," he asked, "why couldn't you come to my party?"

"I didn't have an answer," she says, crying at the memory. "I hurt him and I hurt him bad. It all came because I wanted to sit at that f—— table!"[80]

The gambling industry defends itself

Many gambling critics say that the industry—including the states that run lotteries—should do more to help compulsive gamblers. They claim that the gambling industry is creating millions of victims by selling gambling as easy and fun. Even more objectionable, they say, is the use of cartoon characters in state lottery advertising, thus making gambling more attractive to children. "When the cigarette industry did this with Joe Camel," says one expert, "the country was outraged. Now our government is doing it."[81]

But the gambling industry denies that it is being irresponsible. Casino owners point to signs in their establishments warning customers to "Bet with your head, not over it." Lottery officials, too, are careful to add a "play responsibly" tag at the end of their commercials.

The head of the American Gaming Association, Frank Fahrenkopf, also denies that problem gamblers make a real difference in casino revenue. "Casinos don't target compulsives," he insists. "They are targeting repeat customers. This is a very competitive business; people can't continue gambling if they are compulsives. They eventually lose all their money."[82]

Other gambling proponents argue that too much is made about people supposedly being innocent victims. They say that the American people are much smarter than the antigambling lobby thinks. "I tell you that there are no suckers in a casino," says Mirage owner Steve Wynn. "It implies ignorance, and

Steve Wynn, owner of the Mirage in Las Vegas, believes that casino patrons know the odds and understand the risks of gambling.

more importantly it implies that there's a predator involved, which has to be me. All you have to do is find one customer at the Mirage who can't tell you what the house percentage is against him, find one person there who's there to make a living, who thinks they can win in the casino as a matter of fact as opposed to being pure luck."[83]

Despite disagreement about the extent of compulsive gambling in the United States, the National Coalition on Problem Gambling has worked hard to gain concessions from the gambling industry. State lotteries, for example, are required to set aside a certain amount of their profits to be used for the treatment of problem gamblers, for informational advertising explaining how to bet within one's limits, and for education in schools. Even so, say critics, the $20 million allotted to address the problem of compulsive gambling is very small compared with the more than $36 billion annually netted by the gambling industry.

Epilogue

GAMBLING IN MANY forms is today not only legal in the United States but socially acceptable. The possibility of banning the activity is remote: It is a large industry, and too many people depend on that industry for their jobs. Gambling is not a genie, say experts, that can be put back into its bottle.

Even so, many gambling experts predict changes in the coming years that will affect not only the kinds of gambling available, but the media in which it is offered. For instance, Internet gambling is a hot topic today, in both political and gambling circles.

Cybergambling

The rapid growth of the Internet over the past few years has resulted in a tremendous number of new opportunities for people. Not only can they access information easily about millions of topics and do their banking on-line, they can also purchase anything from stocks and bonds to baby-shower gifts. One of the most controversial opportunities available in cyberspace is Internet gambling.

The vast size of the Internet (20 million sites and growing) makes regulation difficult. Realizing it would be nearly impossible to control it, the federal government in 1995 stopped trying and left oversight of the Internet to its participants.

Internet gambling has been popular since 1994, when the first cybercasino opened its website. No one knows for certain the exact number of online gambling sites, but at least nine hundred advertise widely, offering games such as blackjack, roulette, and slot machines. And although online betting is only a fraction of the U.S. gambling industry, its growth has been very impressive. Revenues for the year 2000 were estimated at $2.2 billion—up from $300 million in 1997.

"The Internet has no boundaries"

This trend disturbs many Americans. Gambling has already become so easy and so acceptable, they say, since the proliferation of lotteries and casinos. Now, anyone with a credit card, a computer, and a modem can place bets online.

"The great concern is that everybody who has access to the Internet will have a video gambling machine sitting in

front of them," says Wisconsin attorney general James Doyle. "By all measures, these kinds of machines are the most addictive and the least social."[84]

Some politicians advocate laws that would make it illegal for Americans to bet money in online casinos, but enforcing such a law would be very difficult, they admit, particularly when a number of cybercasinos originate in other countries, beyond the jurisdiction of American laws. One offshore site located in Antigua accepted $200 million in sports wagers in 1999—95 percent of which came from U.S. bettors. "One hundred bets a minute," boasts the owner, Steve Schillinger. "You get people betting from New York, Chicago, Atlanta, and all over the country."[85]

Two main concerns about online betting are that it is too accessible to minors and too easily abused by compulsive or problem gamblers. But limiting gambling operations such as Schillinger's would be a legal nightmare, says one law professor: "Physical boundaries matter a great deal in the real world. The challenge is that we live in a legal world that has boundaries, but the Internet has no boundaries."[86]

Can the gambling boom survive?

While it is true that gambling has become common and readily accessible in the United States, there are some who maintain that it is only a matter of time before its popularity will decline. Legalized gambling has been running on a seventy-year boom-and-bust cycle since the colonists started the first lotteries. The trend historically has reversed after twenty to thirty years, when people get fed up and embrace more conservative values.

Others say that, values aside, the economy won't long tolerate today's high levels of gambling. With so many gambling options open to them close to home, people may not be as willing to cross the country to Las Vegas casinos. Unfortunately for states, it is only out-of-state gamblers who provide the "healthy" money to casinos—local gamblers are spending money at the casino that they would ordinarily

spend elsewhere in the state. That kind of gambling doesn't help state economies at all.

"Gambling is only a transfer of wealth," insists one expert. "You're taking money away from refrigerators, car payments, mortgages, and putting it into a casino. The problem with people who support casinos is that they're only looking at one side of the equation."[87]

The future of the gambling boom is an open question.

But gambling experts have scorned such predictions. People enjoy gambling, they say, and they're not going to stop—not at the rate they're going now. And a downturn in the industry seems unlikely. In light of the popularity of the easy-maintenance video poker and slot machines, *not* making money seems impossible to casino owners.

Says one owner, "It's like spitting and missing the floor."[88]

Notes

Introduction

1. Personal interview, name withheld, Richfield, MN, July 1, 2000.
2. Telephone interview, Barbara, July 3, 2000.
3. Personal interview, Monica, Shakopee, MN, July 26, 2000.
4. James Popkin and Katia Hetter, "America's Gambling Craze," *U.S. News & World Report*, March 14, 1994, p. 42.
5. Personal interview, name withheld, Shakopee, MN, July 26, 2000.
6. Quoted in Stephen Longstreet, *Win or Lose: A Social History of Gambling in America.* Indianapolis: Bobbs-Merrill, 1977, p. ix.

Chapter 1: Our Gambling Heritage

7. Quoted in Longstreet, *Win or Lose*, p. 31.
8. Quoted in Longstreet, *Win or Lose*, p. 31.
9. Quoted in Longstreet, *Win or Lose*, p. 37.
10. Quoted in Longstreet, *Win or Lose*, p. 36.
11. J. M. Fenster, "Nation of Gamblers," *American Heritage*, September 1994, p. 34 ff.
12. Quoted in Herbert Asbury, *Sucker's Progress: An Informal History of Gambling in America from the Colonies to Canfield.* Montclair, NJ: Patterson Smith, 1969, pp. 72–73.
13. Quoted in Asbury, *Sucker's Progress*, p. 73.
14. Rod L. Evans and Mark Hance, eds., *Legalized Gambling: For and Against.* Chicago: Open Court, 1998, p. 114.
15. Quoted in Asbury, *Sucker's Progress*, p. 79.
16. Quoted in Editors of Time-Life Books, *The Gamblers.* Alexandria, VA: Time-Life, 1978, p. 55.
17. Longstreet, *Win or Lose*, p. 45.
18. Quoted in Editors of Time-Life, *The Gamblers*, p. 61.

19. Ann Fabian, *Card Sharps, Dream Books & Bucket Shops: Gambling in 19th-Century America*. Ithaca, NY: Cornell University Press, 1990, p. 6.

Chapter 2: The Dawning of Gambling's Modern Age

20. Quoted in Timothy O'Brien, *Bad Bet: The Inside Story of the Glamour, Glitz, and Corruption in the World's Largest City*. New York: Times Business, 1998, p. 24.

21. Quoted in Asbury, *Sucker's Progress*, p. 87.

22. Quoted in Asbury, *Sucker's Progress*, p. 87.

23. Robert K. DeArment, *Knights of the Green Cloth: The Saga of the Frontier Gamblers*. Norman: University of Oklahoma Press, 1982, p. 389.

24. Quoted in DeArment, *Knights of the Green Cloth*, p. 390.

25. Quoted in DeArment, *Knights of the Green Cloth*, p. 392.

26. Quoted in Editors of Time-Life, *The Gamblers*, p. 232.

27. Quoted in Jennifer Vogel, ed., *Crapped Out: How Gambling Ruins the Economy and Destroys Lives*. Monroe, ME: Common Courage, 1997, p. 2.

28. Quoted in Longstreet, *Win or Lose*, p. 10.

29. O'Brien, *Bad Bet*, p. 30.

30. Ovid Demaris, *The Boardwalk Jungle*. New York: Bantam, 1986, p. 2.

31. Quoted in O'Brien, *Bad Bet,* p. 70.

Chapter 3: Indian Casinos

32. Quoted in David Segal, "Dances with Sharks," *Washington Monthly*, March 1992, p. 28.

33. Quoted in Segal, "Dances with Sharks," p. 28.

34. Quoted in Joe Coombs, "Ledyard, Conn.–Area Casinos Cash in on Profits," *Knight-Ridder/Tribune Business News*, August 23, 1999, p. 19.

35. Personal interview, Lloyd, Shakopee, MN, July 26, 2000.

36. Quoted in Coombs, "Ledyard, Conn.–Area Casinos," p. 19.

37. Quoted in John Grund, "Shuffling the Deck: Indian-Owned Casinos in Oregon," *Oregon Business*, February 1997, p. 26.

38. Quoted in Jan Golab, "In the Chips: Indian Casinos in California," *Los Angeles Magazine*, December 1999, p. 50.

39. Quoted in O'Brien, *Bad Bet*, p. 142.

40. Quoted in James Popkin, "Gambling with the Mob?" *U.S. News & World Report*, August 23, 1993, p. 30.

41. O'Brien, *Bad Bet*, p. 143.

42. Quoted in Richard Worsnop, "Gambling Boom," *CQ Researcher*, March 18, 1994, p. 241.

43. Quoted in Miriam Davidson, "Hopis Balk at Blackjack, Dance to Different Drum," *Christian Science Monitor*, April 19, 1995, p. 3.

44. Daniel D'Ambrosio, "Incident at Akwesasne," *Gentlemen's Quarterly*, November 1993, p. 216.

45. D'Ambrosio, "Incident at Akwesasne," p. 216.

46. Quoted in Elizabeth Manning, "Gambling: A Tribe Hits the Jackpot," *High Country News*, April 1, 1996, p. 1.

47. Quoted in Ruth Denny, "Indian Casino Hits Jackpot," *Utne Reader*, November/December 1992, p. 35.

48. Ben Nighthorse Campbell, "The Foxwoods Myth," *New York Times*, March 29, 1995, p. 23A.

Chapter 4: Is Gambling a Good Bet?

49. David Johnston, *Temples of Chance: How America Inc. Bought Out Murder Inc. to Win Control of the Casino Business,* Garden City, NJ: Doubleday, 1992, p. 14.

50. Quoted in Vogel, *Crapped Out*, p. 4.

51. Personal interview, Ray, Shakopee, MN, July 26, 2000.

52. Quoted in James Popkin, "Tricks of the Trade," *U.S. News & World Report*, March 14, 1994, pp. 48ff.

53. O'Brien, *Bad Bet*, p. 4.

54. Quoted in Popkin, "Tricks of the Trade," p. 48ff.

55. O'Brien, *Bad Bet*, p. 79.

56. Quoted in Michael Angeli, "Fleecing Las Vegas," *Esquire*, May 1997, p. 63ff.

57. David Spanier, "The Joy of Gambling," *Wilson Quarterly*, Autumn 1995, pp. 34ff.

58. Spanier, "The Joy of Gambling," pp. 34ff.

59. Quoted in Robert Goodman, *The Luck Business: The Devastating Consequences and Broken Promises of America's Gambling Explosion*. New York: Martin Kessler, 1995, p. 39.

60. Quoted in Goodman, *The Luck Business*, p. 19.

61. Quoted in Vogel, *Crapped Out*, p. 2.

62. Quoted in Goodman, *The Luck Business*, p. 91.

63. Quoted in Peter Keating, "Lotto Fever: We All Lose!" *Money*, May 1996, pp. 142ff.

64. Quoted in Goodman, *The Luck Business*, p. 10.

65. Johnston, *Temples of Chance*, p. 15.

66. Quoted in Goodman, *The Luck Business*, p. 47.

Chapter 5: When Gambling Becomes a Problem

67 Quoted in Catherine Edwards, "Legal Gambling May Be a Bad Bet," *Insight on the News*, May 31, 1999, p. 18.

68. Quoted in Blake Hurst, "The Government as Gambling Partner," *American Enterprise*, March/April 1996, p. 62.

69. Quoted in Hurst, "The Government as Gambling Partner," p. 62.

70. Quoted in John W. Kennedy, "Gambling Away the Golden Years," *Christianity Today*, May 24, 1999, pp. 40ff.

71. Personal interview, Mabel, Shakopee, MN, July 26, 2000.

72. Quoted in O'Brien, *Bad Bet*, p. 58.

73. Personal interview, name withheld, Bloomington, MN, July 16, 2000.

74. Personal interview, name withheld, Minneapolis, MN, August 1, 2000.

75. Quoted in Matea Gold and David Ferrell, "Going for Broke," *Los Angeles Times*, December 13, 1998, p. 1A.

76. Personal interview, Sheri, Minneapolis, MN, August 2, 2000.

77. Quoted in Gold and Ferrell, "Going for Broke," p. 1A.

78. Quoted in Goodman, *The Luck Business*, p. 48.

79. Quoted in Gold and Ferrell, "Going for Broke," p. 1A.

80. Quoted in Gold and Ferrell, "Going for Broke," p. 1A.

81. Quoted in Gold and Ferrell, "Going for Broke," p. 1A.

82. Quoted in O'Brien, *Bad Bet*, p. 46.

83. Quoted in O'Brien, *Bad Bet*, p. 45.

Epilogue

84. Quoted in O'Brien, *Bad Bet*, pp. 15–16.

85. Quoted in O'Brien, *Bad Bet*, p. 15.

86. Quoted in "Offshore Betting: The Feds Are Rolling Snake Eyes," *Business Week*, August 28, 2000, p. 71.

87. Quoted in "Offshore Betting," p. 71.

88. Quoted in Coombs, "Ledyard, Conn.–Area Casinos," p. 19

Organizations
to Contact

American Gaming Association
555 13th Street NW, Suite 1010 East
Washington, DC 20003-1109
website: www.americangaming.org

This association represents the gaming-entertainment industry by addressing regulatory, legislative, and educational issues. The association serves as a clearinghouse for information, develops aggressive educational and advocacy programs, and provides leadership in addressing industry issues that are of public concern, such as problem and underage gambling.

Institute for the Study of Gambling and Commercial Gaming
College of Business Administration, University of Nevada
1664 N. Virginia Street
Reno, NV 89957
website: www.unr.edu/colleges/coba/game

The institute offers courses and degrees in management and other areas of gambling. It holds national and international conferences on gambling and publishes minutes of proceedings. The institute publishes books and reports on current issues and trends in legalized gambling and copublishes, with the National Council on Problem Gambling, the *Journal of Gambling Studies*.

National Coalition Against Legalized Gambling (NCALG)
110 Maryland Avenue NE
Washington, DC 20002
website: www.ncalg.org

NCALG opposes the gambling industry and fights for federal laws curtailing it. It also provides research and technical support to grassroots groups that battle the expansion of gambling in their states.

National Council on Problem Gambling
John Jay College of Criminal Justice
445 West 59th Street
New York, NY 10019
website: www.ncpgambling.org

The organization includes health, education, and law professionals, recovering gamblers, and others concerned with compulsive gambling. It conducts seminars and training programs on the identification and treatment of compulsive gambling and behavior. It also publishes books, brochures, videos, and the quarterly *National Council on Problem Gambling* newsletter.

National Indian Gaming Association (NIGA)
224 Second Street SE
Washington, DC 20003
website: www2.dgsys.com/~niga

NIGA comprises American Indian tribes that operate bingo games or gambling casinos. It works for the successful operation of Indian casinos as well as effective tribal, state, and federal regulation. NIGA publishes the quarterly newsletter *Moccasin Telegraph*.

Suggestions for Further Reading

John Burnham, *Bad Habits: Drinking, Smoking, Taking Drugs, Gambling, Sexual Misbehavior, and Swearing in American History*. New York: New York University Press, 1993. Somewhat difficult reading, but excellent material on poker and other card games.

Charles P. Cozic and Paul Winters, eds., *Gambling*. San Diego: Greenhaven Press, 1995. Excellent bibliography and appendixes.

"Gambling on the Future," 1993, Kurtis Productions and A&E Network. Videotape. Good information about the casinos in Deadwood, South Dakota, and their impact on the town.

Daniel E. Ginsburg, *The Fix Is In: A History of Baseball Gambling and Game Fixing Scandals*. Jefferson, NC: McFarland, 1995. Excellent information about the infamous Black Sox scandal, among others.

Kenneth S. Greenberg, *Honor & Slavery: Lies, Duels, Noses, Masks, Dressing as a Woman, Gifts, Strangers, Humanitarianism, Slave Rebellions, The Proslavery Argument, Baseball, Hunting, Gambling in the Old South*. Princeton, NJ: Princeton University Press, 1996. Excellent information, but somewhat difficult reading. Good source notes.

Norton Mockridge and Robert Prall, *The Big Fix: Graft and Corruption in the World's Largest City*. New York: Henry Holt, 1954. Dated but very interesting view of the payoffs connected with gambling in the 1940s and 1950s.

"The Real Las Vegas" vol. 4 "House of Cards," MPH Entertainment and A&E Network, 1996. Well-researched, well-presented videotape.

Andrew Riconda, ed., *Gambling*. New York: H.W. Wilson, 1995. Interesting anthology of articles about gambling, but lacks index.

Carol Silverman Saunders, *Straight Talk About Teenage Gambling*. New York: Facts On File, 1999. Easy reading; thorough list of gambling help-lines.

Works Consulted

Books

Herbert Asbury, *Sucker's Progress: An Informal History of Gambling in America from the Colonies to Canfield*. Montclair, NJ: Patterson Smith, 1969. Very readable, with good material on lotteries and numbers running.

Robert K. DeArment, *Knights of the Green Cloth: The Saga of the Frontier Gamblers.* Norman: University of Oklahoma Press, 1982. Difficult reading, but fascinating background material about the riverboat gambling industry.

Ovid Demaris, *The Boardwalk Jungle*. New York: Bantam, 1986. Good information on the coming of gambling to Atlantic City.

Editors of Time-Life Books, *The Gamblers*. Alexandria, VA: Time-Life, 1978. Fascinating old photographs, excellent bibliography.

Rod L. Evans and Mark Hance, eds., *Legalized Gambling: For and Against.* Chicago: Open Court, 1998. An anthology with a very well written and informative overview; good index.

Ann Fabian, *Card Sharps, Dream Books & Bucket Shops: Gambling in 19th-Century America*. Ithaca, NY: Cornell University Press, 1990. Describes the social aspects of gambling in the United States during the1800s.

Robert Goodman, *The Luck Business: The Devastating Consequences and Broken Promises of America's Gambling Explosion*. New York: Martin Kessler, 1995. Helpful section on lotteries and states' dependence on them.

David Johnston, *Temples of Chance: How America Inc. Bought Out Murder Inc. to Win Control of the Casino Business*. Garden

City, NJ: Doubleday, 1992. Instructive account about how big business took over the gambling industry from organized crime.

Stephen Longstreet, *Win or Lose: A Social History of Gambling in America.* Indianapolis: Bobbs-Merrill, 1977. Excellent section on the historical corruption in lotteries.

Timothy O'Brien, *Bad Bet: The Inside Story of the Glamour, Glitz, and Danger of America's Gambling Industry.* New York: Times Business, 1998. Extremely well written, informative material on the edge casinos have over gamblers.

Jennifer Vogel, *Crapped Out: How Gambling Ruins the Economy and Destroys Lives.* Monroe, ME: Common Courage, 1997. Interesting mixture of articles; well-written introduction and overview.

Periodicals

Michael Angeli, "Fleecing Las Vegas," *Esquire*, May 1997.

Ben Nighthorse Campbell, "The Foxwoods Myth," *New York Times*, March 29, 1995.

Joe Coombs, "Ledyard, Conn.–Area Casinos Cash in on Profits," *Knight-Ridder/Tribune Business News,* August 23, 1999.

Daniel D'Ambrosio, "Incident at Akwesasne," *Gentlemen's Quarterly*, November 1993.

Miriam Davidson, "Hopis Balk at Blackjack: Dance to Different Drum," *Christian Science Monitor*, April 19, 1995.

Ruth Denny, "Indian Casino Hits Jackpot," *Utne Reader*, November/December 1992.

Catherine Edwards, "Legal Gambling May Be a Bad Bet," *Insight on the News*, May 31, 1999.

James Fenster, "Nation of Gamblers," *American Heritage*, September 1994.

Jan Golab, "In the Chips: Indian Casinos in California," *Los Angeles Magazine*, December 1999.

Matea Gold and David Ferrell, "Going for Broke," *Los Angeles Times*, December 13, 1998.

John Grund, "Shuffling the Deck: Indian-Owned Casinos in Oregon," *Oregon Business*, February 1997.

Blake Hurst, "The Government as Gambling Partner," *American Enterprise*, March/April 1996.

Peter Keating, "Lotto Fever: We All Lose!" *Money,* May 1996.

John W. Kennedy, "Gambling Away the Golden Years," *Christianity Today*, May 24, 1999.

Elizabeth Manning, "Gambling: A Tribe Hits the Jackpot," *High Country News,* April 1, 1996.

"Offshore Betting: The Feds Are Rolling Snake Eyes," *Business Week*, August 28, 2000.

James Popkin, "Gambling with the Mob," *U.S. News & World Report*, August 23, 1993.

———, "Tricks of the Trade," *U.S. News & World Report*, March 4, 1994.

James Popkin and Katia Hetter, "America's Gambling Craze," *U.S. News & World Report*, March 14, 1994.

David Segal, "Dances with Sharks," *Washington Monthly*, March 1992.

Daniel Spanier, "The Joy of Gambling," *Wilson Quarterly*, Autumn 1995.

Richard Worsnop, "Gambling Boom," *CQ Researcher*, March 18, 1994.

Index

Picture Credits

About the Author

Gail B. Stewart received her undergraduate degree from Gustavus Adolphus College in St. Peter, Minnesota. She did her graduate work in English, linguistics, and curriculum study at the College of St. Thomas and the University of Minnesota. She taught English and reading for more than ten years.

She has written over ninety books for young people, including a series for Lucent Books called The Other America. She has written many books on historical topics such as World War I and the Warsaw ghetto.

Stewart and her husband live in Minneapolis with their three sons, Ted, Elliot, and Flynn; two dogs; and a cat. When she is not writing she enjoys reading, walking, and watching her sons play soccer.